Dark Mind Control Techniques in NLP

The Secret Body of Knowledge in Psychology That Explores the Vulnerabilities of Being Human. Powerful Mindset, Language, Hypnosis, and Frame Control

Emory Green

CLAIM YOUR FREE GIFT

This book comes with a free bonus item.

Head straight to the last chapter to quickly claim your gift today!

TABLE OF CONTENTS

INTRODUCTION

Have you ever been in a situation in which you felt manipulated or influenced to act, behave, or think in a specific way for reasons other than your own? Perhaps your popular friends persuaded you to do something you didn't fully agree with? Has the sample person at the grocery store ever tried to convince you to buy the food they offered you to sample? Or, what if a supposed utility worker tries to persuade you to buy their services at a cheaper rate even if you are not needing those in the first place? What did they do to convince you? Did you consent? Were you even *aware* that you consented?

Truth is, there are highly persuasive and manipulative people out there who are successful in their ability to use NLP for their own advantage. One good example of people who use NLP successfully are salespeople; a case would be a cable company representative having persuaded you to buy more services that you didn't really need. If you are alarmed about the concept of NLP, wondering how it works or are curious why people are interested in harnessing its power, you've come to the right place. NLP can change your life when you put it into practice, and to have it so, you should be exploring the potentials, truths, and controversies of the most powerful NLP techniques. These techniques have been known to transform lives, decisions, and how people think.

NLP, once mastered, draws a roadmap in your mind that can alter it into something that works to help you reach your goals. Accessing the ability to control your mind and other people's to achieve favorable outcomes, while also aligning your programming and beliefs with success, is essential. Once you understand your own concept of control and how to apply these powerful NLP techniques for your own gains without guilt and limiting beliefs, you will be on your way to living the life you've always dreamed of!

Decades into the profession of business psychology, I have seen patterns of the smartest, most cunning mindsets that would not take no for an answer when it came to winning business and life. I have witnessed large corporate deals between leaders looking for favorable outcomes for their business and career. As a business psychologist who draws success roadmaps for people, political campaigns, and businesses, I give these people my applause every time. It is true that some will do anything for success. This is why, more than the usual, psychology of good motives and purpose is needed to be successful with life, goals, and undertakings. I am also passionate about looking into the less-explored side of winning, which includes darker, albeit highly influential, manipulative techniques for persuasion and always getting what one wants.

However, this book does not assert what is right and what is wrong; instead, it will be giving you helpful insights on the power and potential of NLP, so you can use it effectively in your life, no matter how you plan to use it. One thing is sure—the knowledge you will gain about NLP has no holds barred and is geared toward aligning your actions with known methods and techniques in psychology. This will help you analyze people, control situations, and avoid being controlled by the very same tactics. So, if you think someone is playing with your mind or you are prone to be around people who may manipulate your mind, you will surely be better equipped after reading this book.

People are in awe of the many win-win situations, opportunities, and business deals that can occur without knowing if these may have been sealed and secured through techniques used in NLP. You are about to learn those techniques today. I hope that you will also get your own positive shift in life after reading this book and achieve the results you really want from any situation.

The topics and knowledge in this book are presented comprehensively and directed to be applied toward areas in which these techniques are found to have the best potential for success. This book is also written without judgment towards its readers. Let us extend full respect to our human capacity to understand human vulnerabilities, flexibilities, diverse perspectives, and mindsets. In addition, this book does not cover the usual topics in NLP, but the controversial albeit most powerful techniques that have historically found success.

Many of us may not realize, but NLP techniques are widely used to sway people's perceptions, mindsets, and decisions. It is practically everywhere in sales, business, the workplace, management, leadership, politics, and even in meaningful relationships. Knowing little about it is almost equivalent to becoming an eventual victim of the power falling into the wrong hands. It is your choice between being controlled and being in control of every situation you are in. Time to take that power into your own hands!

More people should be well-read, well-aware, and well-informed about the potential power of psychology, and more than those manipulators inclined to use it deviantly and with unbalanced views. Knowledge is *key!* If you want to create a win-win experience for everyone, then you should be the rightful taker of this power now. Read this book and use all its information to create the world you want for you and everyone in it.

Enjoying this book so far? Remember to head to the bottom of this book for a bonus bite-sized yet valuable free resource on Conversational Hypnosis. This mini e-book is the easiest way to learn how to be a successful conversational hypnotist. Curious about the benefits it can do to your normal day to day conversations? Get your copy now! This free resource is available for a limited time only.

CHAPTER ONE:

The Mysteries of NLP

NLP Today

NLP, or **neuro-linguistic programming**, has been evolving over time, as more and more people witness its application in various situations of life, whether that be business, familial, social, or personal. NLP, as an evolving science, can be useful because it allows for changes of people's thoughts, associations, behaviors, and even emotions. NLP can ultimately change a person's life, given the power of suggestion, influence, and persuasion through techniques used to help them find more beneficial ways of thinking and taking action. In short, NLP can be practical and advantageous to any situation, no matter how difficult or challenging.

NLP Interpreted

NLP consists mainly of three important components: the mind or brain; language, including both verbal and non-verbal; and individual programming. The first part of NLP—the **mind** or **neuro**—suggests how different states of mind can affect a person's behavior and communication. For example, if my present state of mind is calm, I will be more likely to communicate effectively, in comparison to if I were stressed and upset. How I think and feel can directly affect the outward manifestation of my functioning and behavior.

The second part of NLP is the **linguistic component** or the **language** an individual employs to communicate their state of mind and body. However, most of us only pay attention to the words spoken rather than non-verbal body language. In fact, it would seem non-verbal communication is more a telltale sign of an individual's state than the words spoken. This is because, while it can be easy to choose words during a verbal interaction, non-verbal body language, like your face flushing, can be more of an involuntary reaction than a choice. In other words, reactions and responses usually do not lie, whereas words can.

The third part of NLP is **programming**. Programming can be described as an individual's customary way of reacting, thinking, feeling, and assuming. However, surviving on autopilot isn't always beneficial when it comes to dealing with new challenges and changes effectively. Change is the capacity to modify or transform into something different, which is where programming comes into the picture. This is because, as human beings, we have the capacity to change our habits to be more beneficial for our purposes and goals. It is a better alternative to following outdated information that no longer serves a purpose. NLP can, in effect, transform people into more functional human beings, given self-modification and adaptation.

Modern Views and Controversies of NLP

Modern views of NLP suggest neuro-linguistic programming is applicable to both businesses and for personal reasons. Businesses can be improved by using NLP techniques cleverly on its employees, buyers, and investors, while an individual can enhance their personal situation by applying NLP techniques to the people in one's life. However, the controversies surrounding NLP stem from the belief that it's a form of brainwashing, hypnosis, and even mind control to get people to do what one wants. This may suggest that people can also be unknowing victims of NLP, such as in modeling, mirroring, and anchoring. For example, when a person skilled in using NLP mirrors or models your use of linguistics and language, the NLP user will create a sense of rapport and trust, thus allowing them to lead the interaction eventually in their favor. In addition, the use of NLP techniques, such as anchoring, can be just as effective in changing subjective experience. This is because, when a skilled NLP user uses anchoring (physically touches the unknowing person), specific states of mind can manifest in the latter, convincing them to act at the NLP user's discretion. This can either lead to positive or negative outcomes, depending on the use of NLP in the situation.

Foundations of NLP

The practice of NLP began in the 1970s with its foundations rooted in psychology, linguistics, and even computer programming, by the means of family therapist Virginia Satir, Gestalt therapist Fritz Perls, and hypnotist Milton Erickson. It was also studied by a group of noteworthy people including linguistic professor John Grinder and computer programming student Richard Bandler. Bandler, Grinder, and others observed that, when therapists like Satir, Perls, and Erickson used particular communication patterns with their clients, more results were achieved in comparison to traditional methods of therapy. For example, when they used modeling—a show that the NLP practitioner values the client through the use of similar predicates, like spoken language—the individual became more prone to letting their guard down and allowing themselves to be led toward more beneficial outcomes.

The foundations of NLP are built on the ability to read an individual through verbal and non-verbal cues. Eye movements, for example, can give away a person's preferences for using feelings, words, or pictures when learning or accessing information. This action allows the NLP user to gauge or estimate such things as the individual's next thought or state of mind. Furthermore, the supporting principles of NLP include building rapport, a full awareness of one's senses, thinking of the outcomes, and a flexibility to adapt to change by implementing new ways of doing things (Bundrant, 2019). The NLP user can then influence any associated behavior, thoughts, and even the emotions by using supporting principles of NLP.

7

Real World Relevance of NLP

The real world relevance of NLP is that it can be used to create successful people and outcomes that benefit, not only the individual, but also everyone associated with them, whether that be employees, colleagues, friends, or family. For example, competing businesses can apply NLP techniques to train their managers and supervisors, which would then teach those employees how to be successful through such practices. In fact, NLP is used widely today because, as businesses become more competitive given the prevalence of the Internet, customer interactions are becoming highly valued. Customer interactions have more influence than an impersonal email from a food delivery service online, for example. It is the influential and persuasive interactions between a business and customer that can determine the fate of the business' success. Therefore, the practice of NLP can increase successful outcomes for all parties involved due to the power of suggestion, persuasion, and influence toward buying a product or service.

Power of NLP

NLP can change lives with repeated practice of reprogramming belief systems, thinking patterns, and outward manifestations of behavior. It can change how you view your present situation to how you react and respond to it. NLP can change the individual's subjective experience of reality, whether that be for better or for worse. More specifically, NLP can influence people on a massive scale with the power of subliminal messaging and interjected layered meaning through powerful NLP techniques like NLP hypnosis and the use of non-specific language to elicit action. For example, the advertising you see everyday can influence you to spend more money than you usually would, due to some of NLP's covert techniques. This, of course, has me wondering if individuals in general even realize such things as the power of consumerism, thanks to neuro-linguistic programming. NLP can literally change the direction of your life by affecting surrounding people on a deeper level due to NLP's prevalent presence. A lot of people likely employ NLP techniques without them realizing it; for example, with the use of emojis in instant messaging to keep a certain mood within the message.

NLP Training

People who take NLP training can become better communicators, more adept at interpreting the nonverbal signals, and more proficient in mastering thoughts and feelings. People also take NLP training to achieve success, whether that be personal or professional. In addition, NLP training can correct less-than-useful behaviors in individuals, such as addiction. It can also elicit information from others by allowing the user to communicate efficiently using learned NLP techniques. NLP training is used for an endless list of reasons.

Levels of NLP training include NLP Practitioner, the NLP Master Practitioner, the NLP Trainer, and the NLP Coach, where NLP Practitioner is the beginning level of instruction and NLP Coach is the top level of training available. Once an individual successfully learns one level of NLP training, that person is allowed to graduate to the next level of NLP proficiency. NLP training becomes successive and more in depth as it progresses from one level to the next.

Specifically, the **NLP Practitioner** starts by learning the NLP basics. In addition, the NLP Practitioner learns to apply NLP techniques to everyday situations. When the NLP Practitioner applies the newly learned NLP techniques and tools to their life, the individual can start to learn how NLP is useful to others as well.

The **NLP Master Practitioner** learns more advanced, detailed, and in-depth NLP models and techniques, such as modifying values and belief systems that can pertain better to work, family, and life. In addition, the NLP Master Practitioner also learns improved techniques in communication, including quantum linguistics, which is a system of language that suggests that the human nervous system is powered by the mind's self-talk and created visual images (Miller, n.d.). Furthermore,

9

the NLP Master Practitioner would also learn about **Meta Programs**, which include leading NLP techniques like linguistic negotiation. Taking the master course is critical to changing and improving in all areas of life.

The next level of NLP training is the **NLP Trainer**. By this point, the NLP Trainer should have mastered all critical and advanced NLP techniques and tools. In addition, the NLP Trainer has learned to present themselves with utmost confidence to their audience as they successfully train others in using persuasive and influential skills on a large scale. These training strategies include understanding and analyzing the processes of groups, so they can become influential speakers and presenters. Once the NLP Trainer has mastered these techniques, they should be able to present them successfully to an audience.

The final level of NLP training is the **NLP Coach**. The NLP Coach is now competent in NLP and life coaching via pretalk, information gathering, transformation, and integration (International Neuro-Linguistic Programming Center, n.d.). In addition, the NLP Coach is flexible and can alternate between various NLP models and techniques during a coaching session. The NLP Coach is capable of directing and guiding the client toward a more successful and beneficial outcome, which is the point of NLP.

Harnessing the Power of NLP

Some reasons people would want to harness the power of NLP include personal empowerment and improvements within business. If an NLP user can motivate people to think, act, and behave in a certain manner that aligns with the former's interests and goals, then they can control and manage people effectively for personal and professional gain. However, a good percentage of NLP users want to help people overcome whatever has been hindering them in their personal lives, whether it be depression, phobias, or bad habits. NLP has the power to change the course of our lives through reprogramming people to be more functional and efficient members of society.

However, harnessing the power of NLP requires the individual to not only master NLP techniques, but also master themselves. In other words, an NLP Practitioner cannot be efficient if they don't practice, because harnessing NLP requires more than words; it requires action on the NLP Practitioner's part for a more believable and effective application. To accomplish this, the NLP Practitioner's body language must match the words chosen to impart the message to the client; otherwise, the client will be less likely to view the former as convincing or credible, affecting the outcome of NLP practice. In other words, the NLP practitioner must be able to control and manipulate their person first before trying to accomplish doing so with others.

It would seem that harnessing the power of NLP is a lot like harnessing one's natural resources, such as the mind or body, to make them more effective.

Dark NLP

In some cases, NLP users employ the techniques to control and manipulate others and their situations to the former's advantage and the latter's expense. For example, someone with narcissistic tendencies can get inside the mind of their victim by using the same NLP techniques that benefit people, but more disruptive and covertly, such as feigning interest in the victim to garner their obedience and subservience to a specific agenda. In other words, **dark NLP** can also be used for malicious intents. In the wrong hands, dark NLP could potentially harm a population because those people could be programmed to inflict destruction instead of promoting more helpful intentions and goals.

NLP's Power to Persuade, Influence, and Manipulate

NLP can persuade, influence, and manipulate people into thinking, feeling, and behaving in ways unaligned with their best interests. For example, when an NLP user speaks words in time to the natural heartbeat of the other person (a mind control technique), the mind of the recipient becomes more suggestible (Kumar, 2016) and, therefore, swayed more easily to the will of others. Another mind control technique they could use involves using more suggestible "**hot words**" because they are connected with the preferred senses the recipient uses most. For instance, words and phrases such as *feel this*, *hear this*, and *see this* can induce a more impressionable state of mind.

More Controversies and Criticisms on the Dangers of NLP

There is much controversy surrounding the use of NLP with the various mind control techniques that were mentioned in the previous sections. One criticism of NLP is that it messes with the recipient's head more than it improves their life. NLP users, like Richard Bandler, have made it their life mission to get inside the other person's thoughts, feelings, perceptions, and beliefs by practicing the art of mind control. Yet, people question its authenticity and validity because NLP has often been framed as a pseudoscience or black magic—not an actual field of scientific study. Other controversies stem from how, although NLP may be framed as a pseudoscience, it is still applicable in most facets of life, from professional development to personal growth. These claims come from the results NLP has produced. Be that as it may, NLP is still evolving with much to be discovered.

Chapter Summary

In this chapter, you have learned all about NLP, or neuro-linguistic programming, in addition to some of its main tools and techniques. You have also learned many reasons why people want to harness and train in NLP techniques. Equally important is dark NLP because of its potential in controlling and manipulating people through mind control. To refresh your memory, here are some key points from this chapter:

- NLP is neuro-linguistic programming through the mind, language, and habitual ways of thinking, feeling, and behaving (programming) can alter subjective experience.
- NLP can be useful for business and personal reasons, given the power of suggestion, persuasion, and influence.
- The foundations of NLP include building rapport, a full awareness of one's senses, thinking of the outcomes, and flexibility to adapt to change.
- The real world relevance of NLP is that it can be used to create successful people and outcomes that benefit not only the individual, but also everybody associated with them. This can include employees, colleagues, friends, or family.
- NLP has the power to change lives with the repeated practice of reprogramming belief systems, thinking patterns, and outward manifestations of behavior.
- People who take NLP training can become better communicators, more adept at interpreting nonverbal signals, and better at mastering their own feelings and thoughts.
- Levels of NLP training include NLP Practitioner, NLP Master Practitioner, NLP Trainer, and NLP Coach.
- Reasons for harnessing the power of NLP include personal empowerment and improvement for successful business.
- Dark NLP employs techniques for controlling the mind and manipulating the individual and the situation to their own advantage—at the recipient's expense.
- NLP can also persuade, influence, and manipulate people into thinking, feeling, and behaving in ways unaligned with the recipient's best interests.
- NLP is not without controversy and criticism.

In the next chapter, you will learn all about crossing dangerous boundaries when using NLP.

CHAPTER TWO:

Crossing Dangerous Boundaries

NLP Ethics

The use of NLP is controversial because many of its techniques can be covert and manipulative to the recipient. This is because most of the time the recipient isn't aware that they are being manipulated. For instance, the use of mirroring to elicit acquiescence, trust, and rapport from the individual is questionable because it tricks the individual into thinking the NLP user is similar to them, thus letting their guard down. This tactic and similar kinds of NLP techniques can cross dangerous boundaries because of the chance that the recipient was anchored to a relatively harmful or destructive state afterward. An even scarier and alarming result would be the possibility that the natural programming of the individual was reconstructed unnaturally.

What Is Ethical and Not Ethical in Using NLP?

It's curious to think whether the practice of NLP is ethical, given its purpose to influence and guide others without their knowledge nor the exposure of a hidden agenda. This could be considered an act of subterfuge because the NLP user employs deceit to accomplish their objective. The recipient can also be viewed as potentially being used as a means to an end. This idea is inherently unethical because the recipient is less in control of their own faculties and decisions when under the influence of NLP, given having been "programmed" subconsciously.

Knowing this information, people who practice NLP should be careful with its use and application, so as not to harm the recipient. The highest standards and ethics would have to be applied, similar to doctors promising to cause no harm to the individual under the Hippocratic oath. Practicing NLP ethically is using it without the intent to harm, control, or otherwise disadvantage others. One's moral compass, whether professional or personal, must be applied to avoid mistreatment of the recipient. In addition, it is more acceptable to practice NLP on yourself to improve your situation more than it is to practice it on others without their consent or knowledge. Subliminal messaging and NLP programming are everywhere—in self-help classes, advertising, business, and even politics.

Are NLP Impositions Ethical?

Advertising, business, and politics are infamous for imposing their views, thoughts, and beliefs onto the recipient. However, a person who professionally engages in NLP practice must steer clear of imposing personal views, values, and beliefs on a suggestible individual because the latter would be more likely to adopt or subscribe to the NLP Practitioner's views when they need an anchoring point for change and unfamiliar territory (InspiritiveNLP, 2008). For example, when my son was deployed to Africa by the Marines for six months, I needed context to deal with not knowing if he or I would survive that experience. I went to see a professional to deal with it, and the professional did not impose her beliefs, values, or views into my person and, as a result, I felt more uninhibited to be myself in discussing my emotions associated with my son being deployed.

However, deployment of NLP techniques is more ethical if the recipient is profoundly aware of what is going on and has given permission ahead of time. This permits the NLP Practitioner to practice their craft ethically and morally, with the intent of improving or bettering the client's situation. Due to the power being entrusted in the NLP Practitioner's hands, they have a responsibility not to abuse the implicit trust granted to them. It is an obligation to the client for the NLP Practitioner to embody integrity when engaging in NLP practice and application with the client. Clearly, similar values and moral principles must guide the conduct of the NLP Practitioner too.

NLP Presuppositions

NLP practice and application include many assumptions that help guide, structure, and define this evolving science into a more ethically accepted line of work. For example, the NLP presupposition of respecting the other person's worldview or model infers that the NLP Practitioner takes into consideration worldviews other than their own. Every worldview or model from which the individual operates should be as worthy and valid as the next. It is important to pay attention to this because, in some cases, the NLP Practitioner may develop their own preconceived ideas about the client based on that worldview, which isn't ethically correct or fair to the recipient.

In fact, it would seem having preconceived notions, ideas, or presuppositions may suggest an inflexibility on the NLP Practitioner's part, leading to another presupposition of NLP practice. According to Goodman, when NLP Practitioners become inflexible in their thinking and communication with the client, rapport isn't as easily forthcoming from the latter (2018). The client may even become resistant to the NLP Practitioner's attempts to build that rapport. Furthermore, ethics starts to enter the conversation because it brings with it an obvious inequality within the equation. It implies an expectation that the client needs to accept all communication from the NLP Practitioner, while neglecting any expectation that the NLP should listen to the client's thoughts and ideas at all. In short, communication and interaction needs to go both ways between the client and the NLP Practitioner because the relationship needs to build a connection of understanding. Despite this give and take, presuppositions can clearly characterize and type what can sometimes be an already unequal balance of power and influence.

Another important presupposition of NLP is that all behaviors have positive intentions because they are the best possible choices at the time, given the availability of resources. In short, we do the best we can with what we have within any given time frame. The behavior is characterized as positive because there is always something useful to be gained (Goodman, 2018). In addition, the behavior is never fundamentally "wrong" due to the aforementioned reasons; however, there is a difference between positive and what is morally acceptable, along with what is negative compared to that which is considered wrong. For instance, if there is something useful to be gained from the practice of NLP, does this infer that the NLP Practitioner's conduct is always positive and ethically acceptable? Clearly, there are presuppositions and assumptions in NLP that seem to be at odds with its actual practice when the tables are turned on the NLP Practitioner and their line of work. This idea contradicts the veracity of NLP practice because of the imbalance of power, persuasion, and influence between the NLP Practitioner and the individual.

Despite this, influencing each other's mind and body leads into the NLP presupposition that one will affect the other because they are interconnected. More specifically, when we change our line of thought, our bodies manifest outward what is going on inside our minds. Likewise, how we behave can also modify our innermost feelings and thoughts. The **mind-body connection** can affect our subjective experience of reality, which is useful to NLP practice and application. This is because, if the NLP Practitioner can modify one's natural state or programming after having learned more about how they operate, then the mind and the body can become more in tune with each other, ultimately benefiting the client. The NLP Practitioner can also benefit from the client's mind-body connection because the former can influence the client even more once the latter's mind and body are synchronized.

Some other NLP presuppositions include (Goodman, 2018):

- We are always communicating.
- We already have all the resources we need, or we can create them; therefore, there is no such thing as unresourceful people. There are only unresourceful states of mind.
- The system (person) with the most flexibility (choices) in their behavior will have the most influence on the system.
- People work perfectly.
- Accept the person, change the behavior.
- There is no failure, only feedback.
- Choice is better than no choice.
- All processes should lead to integration and wholeness.
- If you want to understand, act.

These NLP presuppositions are quite valuable to NLP application because they also help guide and direct its real world implementation.

NLP Applications

NLP as an evolving science can be used for various purposes. One of those purposes includes self-improvement into the best version of ourselves. For example, NLP can help a person achieve an optimal state of health by reprogramming them to adopt consistently healthier exercise and eating habits. Perhaps less than healthy habits like smoking could also disappear with a persuasive influence from the NLP practitioner. In the case that an individual wants to communicate better with a loved one, there are many NLP-based self-improvement classes they can take to optimize that situation, among others as well.

In addition, NLP is used for professional and business purposes, such as in teaching how to become a better manager, colleague, or leader through NLP techniques. For example, a manager could learn to communicate better with employees to elicit improved productivity on the job. On the other hand, an employee could potentially improve their mindset so they can understand and work with fellow employees more efficiently. In short, NLP is mostly used for professional and personal enhancement.

However, NLP is also sometimes used to control people on a large scale through content/context reframing at seminars and gatherings. For example, the individual employing NLP on the crowd would reframe the situation as being more optimal than it really is, so they can distract the large group of people from their actual message, usually brainwashing or persuading them into believing whatever ideology, such as Hare Krishna. Another example could be in a large business seminar about improving relationships with customers. With these, the skilled NLP user may indoctrinate the large group into accepting without question the beliefs, values, and perceptions. One method the NLP user would use to accomplish this is to induce a heightened state of suggestibility through layered and subliminal messaging, so they can reframe the situation as more positive or optimal.

In terms of **layered meaning** and **subliminal messaging**, advertisements may also try to trick the consumer into buying their products or services by using certain NLP techniques. For example, using vague language allows the advertiser to trick the consumer into believing that they have more options to choose from because vague language allows for more interpretations of the advertiser's message (Evolution Development, 2019). This emanates from the Milton Model from Milton Erickson, who purposefully used vague language with his clients to allow more room for interpretation. It is this ambiguous language that can make the consumer buy into the product or service, given the supposed freedom of choice presented. NLP practitioners can also present choices to their clients through purposeful, non-specific language.

NLP is also used in politics, especially during election time, when the candidates start airing advertisements directed at the voting populace. Some politicians even go so far as to use **hypnotic trance words** so the voter becomes more likely to feel a sense of rapport with the politician. For example, according to Basu, some words are similar to an anchored trance effect, since they impact us with a meaning we would ascribe through our thoughts, feelings, beliefs, and experiences (2015). When an influential politician repeats these words back to the people, the people then become more motivated than before. This can also affect the voting populace by making them more oblivious to the effects of political maneuvering.

Cults and Manipulators Use and Abuse NLP

Manipulators and cults will use and abuse NLP by overrunning an individual's sense of identity and agency by pushing an unstated agenda with the intention of total mind control, obedience, and subservience. This mind control can be dangerous to the welfare of the individual because thinking or acting independently becomes next to impossible. This impossibility stems from the individual being taught to *depend* on the cult leaders and group for their sense of identity, meaning, and/or purpose. The individual suffers detrimental consequences because that lack of identity allows for easier manipulation and mind control through mass hypnosis. In other words, NLP application among similar techniques by a destructive cult or a manipulator does not help the individual, but instead, harming them. These actions are unethical and dangerous.

Clearly, there is the potential to cross dangerous boundaries when practicing NLP. For instance, the recipient may no longer be able to function effectively in life due to their subjective reality and consciousness having become less functional. Marriages can break down, job loss can occur, and less-than-optimal psychological conditions like depression may even surface after a weekend with NLP enthusiasts. According to Tippet, cult-like groups can use mass hypnosis to bring about a subjectively altered state of mind for the individual by inhibiting the latter's faculties and inducing emotional responses (1994). For example, when I went through Army basic training, the drill sergeants would yell commands to follow, which induced an emotional response, thus attempting to break down the new recruit into submission. It is an

21

effective technique that produces obedience and subservience in the individual because, after following their commands for so long, emotional and physical exhaustion can hinder the original sharpness of the recruit's faculties. Such techniques can be harmful to the recipient because their individuality no longer exists in these circumstances, having been overrun by cult-like techniques reminiscent of hypnosis and NLP. Case in point, after I was honorably discharged from the military, it took some time for me to acclimate back to everyday life again.

As we've seen, NLP and similar techniques can be dangerous to not only the individual, but also the group, which is why NLP techniques need to be practiced and applied with the utmost care and awareness. NLP practitioners must take this responsibility to heart, due to the trust that has been given and sometimes elicited from the client. I believe this quote sums up the situation fully:

> *Nearly all men can stand adversity, but if you want to test a man's character, give him power*
>
> Abraham Lincoln

Chapter Summary

In this chapter, you have learned about the ethics of NLP practice. You have also learned about how the presuppositions of NLP can help guide the practice, while also considering their ethical implications. Furthermore, you have learned about how NLP has been used in other ways beyond self-help. Lastly, we went over the importance of considering how NLP can be abused by organizations such as cults. To refresh your memory, here are some of the key points from this chapter:

- NLP techniques can cross dangerous boundaries, given its covert and manipulative nature.
- In order to keep NLP ethical, it should be used without the intent to harm, control, or otherwise disadvantage others.

- NLP practitioners must not impose their values, perceptions, and beliefs onto the client.
- The NLP practitioner has a responsibility not to abuse the implicit trust granted to them during a session.
- Presuppositions, like respecting the individual, help guide the practice of NLP. Some other presuppositions include (Goodman, 2018):
    - There are no resistant clients, only inflexible communicators.
    - The mind and body affect each other because they are connected.
    - We are always communicating.
    - We already have all the resources we need, or we can create them; therefore, there is no such thing as unresourceful people, only unresourceful states of mind.
    - The system (person) with the most flexibility (choices) in its/their behavior will have the most influence on the system.
    - People work perfectly.
    - Accept the person, change the behavior.
    - There is no failure, only feedback.
    - Choice is better than no choice.
    - All processes should lead to integration and wholeness.
    - If you want to understand, act.
- NLP is used for self-improvement, business, advertising, politics, among other areas.
- NLP can be abused by manipulators and cults, who use it to overrun an individual's sense of identity and agency for easier manipulation and mind control.

In the next chapter, you will learn about the fundamentals of control and manipulation

CHAPTER THREE:

Control and Manipulation

Control and Manipulation Interpreted

Having the power to direct, control, or otherwise manipulate people's thoughts, feelings, and behaviors skillfully is a big deal. This manipulation can affect those people significantly and for a long time, depending on the type, depth, and direction of control and manipulation used. It is the control and manipulation that can shape and influence lives either optimally or nonoptimally. In this case, the person in control can direct and even determine the subjective experience and reality of the person being controlled. In fact, the implications of the controller's outward behavior, words, and actions can directly affect the person being controlled, due to the latter's interpretation and reactions.

Control and manipulation in the context of NLP can be quite similar, with **control** being the power to direct people's behavior, whereas **manipulation** is the action of controlling something skillfully. The main difference between control and manipulation is that having the power to direct something (control) is not the same as knowing how to skillfully do it (manipulation). For example, I have the power to program my computer (control) efficiently, yet I may not know how to skillfully do that (manipulation) quite yet, given a lack of experience or training. It seems being able to manipulate something adeptly, such as a computer, takes the reality of control to the next level.

Being in Control and Being Controlled

Likewise, being *in control* compared to being *controlled* also suggests different subjective realities. More specifically, being in control is an active state compared to being controlled, which is more passive. For example, a skilled psychologist controls or directs the therapy session actively, whereas the client would allow the psychologist to guide them as the recipient of that expertise. In addition, being in control involves agency and autonomy, whereas being controlled usually does not. If I just allowed things to happen to me, I would be more likely to be controlled by others; however, if I take action, I will be more able to control how I respond to those events. The difference is in the response to the stimuli because the individual can react or choose to act instead.

Avoid Being Controlled

To avoid being controlled by a manipulator, it is important to have a strong sense of identity or self. This is because being aware of your identity allows you to be more in-tune with your values, beliefs, and feelings. Your awareness will then allow you to protect yourself from someone trying to impose their beliefs on you using covert manipulation techniques. Manipulators and other controlling people won't be as likely to take advantage and compromise your core identity when you know yourself and what you stand for. Otherwise, taking advantage of someone is easier if that person isn't fully aware of their identity.

Another way to avoid being controlled is to have confidence in yourself. A lack of confidence can lead to self-questioning, thus making you naturally give others more credibility than they deserve (Golden, 2016). The resulting self-doubt will allow controlling people to push their beliefs, values, and agenda on you much easier because you are handing more power over to them. This can lead to becoming a pawn for the manipulator because their validation of your self-worth will give you a false sense of confidence. It is also healthier to build confidence in yourself to begin with.

It is also important to avoid becoming overly dependent on other people so you won't be controlled by them. For example, if you depend on your partner to satisfy your every need instead of engaging in self-care regularly, then you may be opening yourself up to that individual's attempts to control you later down the road. In other words, when you neglect to take care of yourself and your needs, you invite others to do it for you through potentially well-meaning albeit controlling interventions (Bundrant, 2011). It can also lead to an unhealthy codependency, given the need for constant coddling; therefore, it is important to learn how you can rely on yourself, so you can avoid this trap altogether.

Furthermore, you will be easier to control if you are not living in the present. In other words, if you are still focusing your attention on past experiences, then those experiences will end up controlling you emotionally and mentally, despite physically being in the present. Living in the past can diminish your critical faculties and your ability to function because that energy will be hijacking your reactions and responses to the present; you will be more fatigued from trying to coexist in both realities and, consequently, you will be easier to manipulate and control.

Internal Control

Being in control is an entirely different experience from being controlled because you are in the driver's seat and can choose for yourself, in contrast to allowing someone else to make those choices for you. Beyond that, being in control allows you to direct and improve the situation to and in your favor. For example, if I can control my reactions to stress with improved coping techniques, I can direct and guide how I respond to them better. This allows the individual to exercise authority over their own autonomy and self-govern their choices. Internal control usually comes with a goal—if that goal is to lose weight, for instance, the individual would adjust their choices and behavior accordingly. If the goal is changed, the behavior is then modified to reach that new goal.

External Control

Applications of the context of control in regards to people and situations suggest that people, in general, aren't as easy to control when their goals change. In this case, they would no longer need to behave or act in the same manner to achieve that goal. According to Carey, what people want can change, thus allowing for the rules of the game to change as well (2015). This makes people and their situations less able to be manipulated and controlled because they no longer need to act or behave the same as before. Therefore, if a change in behavior, thoughts, and feelings can occur as a result, control is no longer applicable to the situation.

Still, controlling and manipulating people becomes less difficult when the main objectives do not change; although, the behavior associated with that goal must change for it to remain effective. We could think of it as there being more than one way to get from point A to point B. For example, an individual can change and manipulate their thinking and still accomplish the same goal by changing the context to reflect the objective and state of mind better. Thus, the main objective of control and manipulation is change itself.

Taking Control of the Past, Present, and Future

Change resulting from skillful manipulation is necessary to take control of the past, present, and future because, otherwise, we could use the past as an excuse to continue poor behavior. On the other hand, thinking in the present can ultimately affect the future. For example, if I continue to eat food when emotionally upset, I will be less likely to eat healthily in the present when faced with new emotional challenges. This can affect my future because, if I become dependent on food whenever I am emotionally challenged, I could gain a lot of weight and/or compromise my health and quality of life. Therefore, repeating past bad habits does not help because they will keep us anchored to that past. If we can change those past behaviors and use more functional coping mechanisms in the present, our present and future outcomes will sway more in our favor.

In addition to repeating past behaviors, people also tend to react more when dealing with past events. For example, if I become emotionally triggered over something upsetting from my past, I may be less likely to deal with it adequately in the present because my emotions would be overwhelming and dampen my ability to act appropriately. I would also have a harder time learning new skills to use in the present when a trigger materializes again. There needs to be a balance of action and reaction to effectively deal with the past, present, and future. Similarly, controlling and manipulating an individual's actions and reactions can benefit both the present and the future.

According to Firestone, the reality of recreating similar dynamics and environments from our past can also color the present and future (2016). This is because, as people, we tend to favor the familiar compared to the unfamiliar; for example, if an individual grew up in a big family with plenty of siblings, that person may recreate that situation by always having plenty of people around, in contrast to learning how to live alone. Recreating the family dynamic or environment may be undesirable, as it can hinder the individual's progress toward adulthood. In addition, manipulating the present to reflect the past isn't always indicative of future events because, although people like to think they have control, reality often suggests otherwise. Case in point—control is an illusion, whereas skillful manipulation is real, given the latter's production of tangible results and outcomes.

Repeating, reacting to, and recreating the past suggests a lack of control and some level of manipulation because, as children, we had little control over the environment and the dynamics we grew up in. Yet, we have more control now with guiding our situation skillfully, due to the differentiation, autonomy, and agency we gained through adulthood. Once we establish that, we can begin to control, guide, or otherwise manipulate important goals into better outcomes ethically. In fact, experiencing better outcomes suggests that the connotation behind control and manipulation is more positive than most would believe.

Consequences of Triggering the Subconscious of Strangers

Once the individual has the power to control, guide, and manipulate their situation more in their favor, that person can then also trigger the subconscious of strangers by using NLP techniques reminiscent of control and manipulation. For example, psychological manipulation through NLP can provoke mental health conditions, such as depression, within the unconscious mind to alleviate them. Some other examples of triggering the subconscious of others include the use of the following NLP techniques and tools (Beale, 2020):

- Affirmations.
- Amplifying good feelings.
- NLP belief change.
- NLP hypnosis and meditation.
- Modeling.

This list is not exhaustive; the NLP toolkit allows for effective manipulation and control of the client, focusing more on producing tangible results compared to traditional forms of therapy. For example, using affirmations will help keep the client on track when their focus drifts from the main goal. **Affirmations**, like belief and mission statements, can also remind the client of their motivation for taking action. In addition, affirmations used correctly can influence mindsets with the use of repetition and reiteration. Therefore, mindful manipulation of thoughts and feelings through affirmation statements can control real life events for the recipients, as it helps them replace negative messages they may have encountered previously.

Amplifying good feelings of clients can also help them strengthen their appreciation of certain events, allowing them to relive those good feelings in vivid detail as well. For example, if I close my eyes and remember the day my son was born, I can envision the sights, sounds, and positive feelings of the moment he was placed in my arms. Nothing compares to holding your firstborn for the first time! The only drawback is that, eventually, the client has to come back to reality and they may have a less-than-positive reaction to coming back. Strangers can benefit from amplifying good feelings, but what if these techniques are misused to control the client maliciously?

In addition, **belief change** is another helpful NLP technique that modifies beliefs to help free up behavior. The philosophy is that, once the recipient realizes their beliefs—even strong ones—are relative and not a scientific truth, those beliefs should have a lesser effect on their behavior. The scary thing is that, if the NLP Practitioner practiced belief change on a stranger on the streets, the stranger's freed-up behavior would be disadvantageous for everyone involved. In this case, behavior becomes unpredictable when beliefs and values do not govern it to some extent. Furthermore, if NLP Practitioners freed up everybody's beliefs through NLP belief change, there would be many people merely doing what they wanted, no matter how chaotic. As implied, this scenario could cause situations akin to anarchy, given the lack of belief systems, thus the lack of control overall.

Nevertheless, practicing NLP hypnosis and meditation is another technique that can trigger the subconscious of strangers. This is accomplished by inducing involuntary control over their faculties while making them highly suggestible to external influences, such as the NLP Practitioner's voice. For example, the client might be able to relax more during the recall of a traumatic life event if the NLP Practitioner uses a specific tone of voice. NLP hypnosis is mainly used to improve the outcomes of NLP therapy, yet when a stranger's subconscious is triggered by hypnosis, they could react negatively to less beneficial influences, thus compromising their identity while hypnotized. Could somebody under NLP hypnosis be responsible for breaking the law? Who is really in control while hypnotized?

Last but not least, the NLP **modeling** technique is also valuable in NLP practice because, by imitating and copying successful methods, it becomes easier to see what works for the individual (Beale, 2020). For example, by imitating and internalizing my mother's work ethic, it will be easier for me to figure out what work ethics work for me within specific jobs and lifestyles. If the client is able to identify with another's success story, then the former will be more likely to want to succeed as well. However, the price paid for modeling another's successful techniques is that the recipient may lose some individuality. The last thing the NLP Practitioner should want is for the recipient to lose their sense of identity and agency. For example, a recipient may lose functioning in their triggered subconscious if they lose their identity.

NLP Mind Control: The Basic Three

The aforementioned NLP techniques can trigger the subconscious of strangers while controlling and manipulating them toward improved life outcomes. According to Lee, NLP mind control techniques, such as changing your physiology, can also affect how you think (2020) and feel. For example, if you want to exude confidence, start by controlling your body language to manifest that confidence outwardly. This will result in your mind eventually picking up on that display in reality. If I want to exude affection, I would physically hug my partner in the hopes that we can both feel that affection in reality. Controlling and manipulating your physiology can produce or elicit the desired state of mind. However, on the dark side of the coin, exuding an unfavorable state of mind does not usually produce the outcomes you want.

The second NLP mind control technique is vocally emphasizing **keywords** in a conversation (Lee, 2020). Doing this helps convince the other person to do something you want, given the point of emphasis. For example, if you stress the keyword, "do" in "do the dishes," the recipient of your command will be more likely to abide by and follow the directive. Emphasizing keywords is also an effective advertising tool. For example, the Nike slogan, "Just do it" emphasizes the keyword "do" to get you to take action. NLP mind control techniques run rampant in society, given their presence in nearly everything, from advertising to politics.

The third NLP mind control technique is **visualization** (Lee, 2020). Visualization is powerful because, when you imagine yourself achieving something, you are more likely to adhere to that path of success than if you hadn't. For example, if I visualize myself succeeding in my career aspirations, I will more than likely triumph in my field. Visualization helps the client picture the goal more clearly, especially if visual cues are the client's preferred form of communication. It is important to note, however, that since some societies are more visual than others, they tend to judge success based on appearances, which is not accurate nor representative.

Clearly, control and manipulation can take many prevalent forms that we don't even recognize, for good or bad. This is when one must actively take control of the situation and manipulate the outcome for the better; otherwise, we can become passive victims to mind control on a massive scale. Nevertheless, the real power comes from the individual controlling and manipulating their past and present to ensure the future is better for everyone.

"Those who control the present, control the past and those who control the past control the future."

George Orwell

Chapter Summary

In this chapter, you have learned about the fundamentals of control and manipulation. In addition, you have also learned about being in control compared to being controlled. It is important to remember to take control of the past, present, and future to achieve success in life. Still, control and manipulation wouldn't be possible without effective NLP techniques to trigger people's subconscious. Lastly, people's subconscious can be controlled and manipulated by NLP mind control. To refresh your memory, here are the key points of this chapter:

- The main difference between control and manipulation is that having the power to direct something (control) is not the same as knowing how to do it skillfully (manipulation).
- Control is an active state compared to being controlled, which is passive.
- Being in control suggests agency, whereas being controlled does not.
- To avoid being controlled by a manipulative person, the individual can:
  o Have a strong sense of identity.
  o Have confidence in oneself.
  o Avoid being overly dependent.
  o Live in the present.
- Being in control allows the individual to exercise authority over their own autonomy and self-govern their choices.
- The rules of the game change when the person no longer wants the same thing. Their behavior would change to accommodate a different goal, making them less likely to be controlled.
- To take control of the past, present, and future, a person must be willing to change by refusing to:
  o Repeat past, nonadaptive behaviors.
  o React more than act.
  o Recreate past relationships and dynamics in the present.
- The skilled NLP Practitioner can trigger the subconscious of strangers by practicing control and manipulation type NLP techniques. Some of those techniques include (Beale, 2020):
  o Affirmation.
  o Amplifying good feelings.
  o NLP belief change.
  o NLP hypnosis and meditation.
  o Modeling.

- Some NLP mind control techniques include:
  - Changing your physiology to affect how you think.
  - Emphasizing keywords in a conversation.
  - Visualization.

In the next chapter, you will learn how to read and control people.

CHAPTER FOUR:

Reading and Controlling People

NLP Mind Reading

Reading a person's mind is about more than going to a psychic medium. It is a science containing methods that NLP Practitioners can use to understand *how* a person is thinking, not necessarily *what* they are thinking. For example, an NLP Practitioner can read a person's body language to determine their state of mind. Reading people through body positions and movements can be helpful in personal, friend, and business relationships, because it helps us not only communicate better, but also estimate the next move in that relationship. For example, if I am frustrated with my partner for whatever reason, furrowing my brows can express to them my frustrations. As a result, my partner's next move would usually be to ask me what's wrong. This interaction would then, in turn, propel the relationship forward. The facts are that my partner and I can read each other at any time, resulting in a healthy, interdependent relationship full of life. Clearly, reading people can produce positive outcomes!

NLP Mind Reading Through Body Language and Eye Accessing Cues

NLP mind reading through **body language** and **eye accessing cues** is helpful for both the NLP Practitioner and the client during sessions because either party can benefit the other. For example, the NLP Practitioner can use the client's body language to determine the latter's best course of action much easier than if they were merely using other traditional methods. In addition, the client would also benefit from the reading because they would learn healthier coping methods by following the NLP Practitioner's lead. Actually, it could even appear that the NLP Practitioner is following the *client's* lead in terms of the latter's subjective state of mind, body language, and eye accessing cues expressed. Both references for mind reading would help indicate the client's reality.

In addition, NLP mind reading is a combination of not only the science behind reading and interpreting body language and eye accessing cues, but also the NLP Practitioner's intuition. The ability to understand something right away can lead to improved directions and guidance during NLP therapy, as the NLP Practitioner would be able to respond quickly and appropriately to the client's body language and eye accessing cues. If the NLP Practitioner can accurately interpret the client's state of mind by the means of NLP mind reading, then there is a higher chance of success for all parties involved within this evolving practice.

Understanding Body Language in NLP

NLP mind reading through body language and eye accessing cues is done across various fields, in addition to NLP itself. For example, police detectives may employ the skill of reading body language to determine whether a criminal is lying, or if the former is making progress during interrogation. Beyond that, body language can still give people an impressive amount of information in terms of their current thoughts and feelings. The majority of that information is non-verbal; according to Bradberry, 55% of communication comes from body language, whereas 38% comes from vocal tone and only 7% comes from the actual words used during an interaction (2017). It is obvious that 55% is a big deal because it can give insight into the nature of human beings themselves.

This is useful for many people in positions of influence. Some the body language that is easier to understand includes (Bradberry, 2017):

- Crossed arms and legs.
- Smiles that crinkle the eyes.
- Copying other people's body language.
- Posture.
- Eyes.
- Raised eyebrows.
- Clenched jaw.

Body language, like crossed arms and legs, suggests the individual is opposing your thoughts and viewpoints actively, while also refusing to be receptive to them. Important to note is that, even if their facial expression suggests happiness through a big smile, they may actually be isolated or disconnected from the other person's ideas, a situation in which they would be physically, emotionally, and mentally closed off. Crossed arms and legs may also signal the need for protection from the other individual's expressed ideas and/or feelings.

One form of body language that can be read easily through NLP practice and has been mentioned briefly is a person's smile. If a person smiles genuinely during a situation, you would see eyes crinkling to follow suit. In fact, the individual would not be seen smiling genuinely if their smile "doesn't reach their eyes," as the saying goes. A person's smile often infers approval, pleasure, or amusement, except in the case when a person is trying to hide something, like emotional or mental pain—in those cases, you might see a smile without eye crinkling. If crow's feet can't be seen around the corners of the eyes, that individual is not really *smiling*.

If someone is copying your body language, it suggests that person can feel a connection with you; therefore, they demonstrate a mirror effect. For example, if my friend smiles in a certain way, I may smile in the same manner. The action of doing so suggests the relationship is going well, and that I am happy to spend time with my friend. In addition, copying body language can entice the other person to open up to you, depending on the body language you use at that moment. An understanding of this concept can be helpful in NLP practice.

An individual's posture can also tell us a multitude of things, such as whether the person is feeling confident or tired; someone with a puffed out chest would impart that they have, or believe they have, power, whereas a slouch would suggest the individual feels less powerful. Having a decent posture is valuable because such a stance can also communicate respect from others. For example, when I was in army basic training, I had to copy or mirror the drill sergeants' body posture to show respect for them, myself, and the uniform.

Another form of body language that is easy to understand include the movement of a person's eyes. If a person purposely holds eye contact with you for a long period of time, then that person could very well be deceiving or outright lying to you. When this is the case, the person's eyes may not blink or move, which suggests that something is amiss. Always pay attention to the eyes. Make note that the average time for holding eye contact is about seven to ten seconds (Bradberry, 2017), so if someone holds eye contact for a longer length of time and starts making you feel uncomfortable, that person could be lying or trying to intimidate you. Recognizing this fact can be quite useful to NLP practice because the NLP Practitioner can figure out if the client is lying to them. Eye movements or lack thereof can communicate various subjective states of mind, among other things.

Raised eyebrows are also a form of body language to pay attention to because they can communicate emotions such as fear, worry, or surprise. For instance, if my friends throw me a surprise birthday party, my initial reaction of surprise when I enter the room may become obvious when my eyebrows elevate to a higher position on my face. Still, raised eyebrows can also suggest something behind the scenes, especially when the topic of discussion should not be eliciting surprise, worry, or fear from the reacting individual. In short, be cautious of raised eyebrows.

Last but not least, a clenched jaw can communicate tension, stress, and discomfort to the other individual during an interaction. For example, I usually clench my jaw when I have to get my blood drawn because the thought of a needle pricking my arm stresses me out. The phlebotomist doing the deed would usually have to distract me by talking to me during a blood draw, so I can relax a bit more and unclench my jaw. Body language communicates a lot of information about the individual, which makes the NLP Practitioner's job easier.

Understanding Eye Accessing Cues in NLP

Also making the NLP Practitioner's job less difficult is reading eye accessing cues from the client during a session. Eye accessing cues, similar to body language, can indicate the client's thoughts, or at least lead the NLP Practitioner in the right direction. In addition, eye accessing cues help the NLP Practitioner determine which representational system the client is accessing. To explain, a **representational system** would include sensory modalities like visual, auditory, or kinesthetic, which are then represented by methods and models that relate how the mind stores and processes information. When an individual uses their mind to think, the NLP Practitioner can determine which representational system they are using to communicate their preferred thinking modality—the NLP Practitioner would then notice these based on eye movements and cues. However, this method does not indicate exactly what the individual is thinking, merely *how* they are thinking. In short, the NLP Practitioner can track the individual's preferred thinking style through those eye movements, which is helpful to NLP processes.

As stated, eye accessing cues assist the NLP Practitioner by communicating whether the client processes information with visuals such as pictures, sounds, and feelings. Pictures are generally anything we can see in reality; sounds can include trickling of running water; and feelings may include happy or upset emotions. Thinking in different ways initiates noticeable changes in the body, and the body would also exert influence on how an individual thinks. For example, how an individual thinks would determine their eye movements, and their eye movements could stimulate various parts of the brain. More precisely, looking up, in terms of NLP movements, is associated with visual thinking, whereas keeping one's eyes level suggests auditory thinking. In addition, looking down is associated with kinesthetic thinking. Looking right or left during these NLP eye movements can determine if the individual is constructing or recalling visuals, sounds, or feelings. Eyes that move to the left indicate the construction of sensory modalities, whereas eyes that look to the right indicate a recall of sensory modalities. NLP eye movements can help the NLP Practitioner understand more about the person and their preferred thinking style.

NLP Accessing Cues: Visual, Auditory, and Kinesthetic

Each representational system has plenty of accessing cues in addition to eye movements and positions. Some other accessing cues include the position of the head and gestures; breathing; and tone, tempo, and pitch of the individual's voice. For example, accessing cues for a visual representation system would include: head up, gestures above the shoulders, breathing in the lungs, and a high-pitched voice with a high tempo of speech. Accessing cues for an auditory representational system would include: head leaning to one side, ear-level gestures, breathing in the diaphragm, and a varied speech tempo and tones. Lastly, accessing cues for a kinesthetic representational system would include: head down, gestures around the body, abdominal breathing, and slower speech with a deeper voice. Given these details about accessing cues and representational systems, people can determine their own preferred representational systems, along with preferred systems in others.

Behavior Indicators of Preferred Representational Systems

In addition, there are behavior indicators that can determine if a person's preferred representational system is visual, auditive, or kinesthetic. For example, there is evidence that I prefer the visual representational system because I tend to be organized, quiet, a decent speller, and I can be very detailed. Some other behavior indicators for visual people include:

- Neat and orderly.
- Observant.
- Appearance-oriented.
- More deliberate.
- Are better at memorizing by picture.

Behavior indicators can determine if an individual prefers the auditory representational system as well; for instance, if the person likes to talk to themselves, says words when reading, speaks in rhythmic patterns, and likes music, then they are probably an auditory person. Some other behavior indicators for auditory people include:

- Learn by listening.
- Talkative.
- Uses a phonetic approach when spelling.
- Enjoys reading out loud.
- Talk better than they write.

Beyond that, behavior indicators for a kinesthetic individual are that the person is generally physically oriented, learns by doing, gestures a lot, and also responds physically to the situation. Other behavior indicators for kinesthetic people include:

- Touch people and stand close.
- Move a lot.
- Larger physical reaction.
- Early large muscle development.
- Learn through manipulation.

Each representational system can help the NLP Practitioner ascertain not only how the individual thinks, but also how they learn, converse, spell, read, write, and imagine. If the NLP Practitioner is keenly aware of how the client thinks, then they will be better able to influence, persuade, or manipulate the client—and the subjective reality experienced—for an improved outcome. Otherwise, it would be much more challenging to help the client with their personal and professional goals.

Controlling People Through Their Preferred Representational System

Controlling people through their preferred representational system is accomplished through the application and practice of NLP techniques and tools that can improve the client's state of mind and change their subjective reality for more practical purposes and functionality. More specifically, the NLP Practitioner can match or mirror the behaviors, movements, and speech of the client, while basing the mirrored actions on the client's preferred representational system. This matching of the client's preferred representational system and the resulting manifestation of it will allow the NLP Practitioner to accommodate, direct, or control the client better. This is because, when the NLP Practitioner assimilates to their client and the latter's preferred representational system, the professional can then improve or change it, with the goal of improved outcomes and success.

Chapter Summary

In this chapter, you have learned about reading and controlling people. You learned that NLP mind reading through body language and eye accessing cues is useful to the application of NLP. It is also important to remember the various representation systems, as they will help both the individual and the NLP Practitioner communicate and understand each other. To refresh your memory, here are the key points of this chapter:

- Reading a person's mind enables the NLP Practitioner to understand how that person is thinking and feeling.
- Reading people allows us to communicate more efficiently.
- NLP mind reading through body language and eye accessing cues is useful because it determines the next course of action in therapy.
- Body language gives people an impressive quantity of information about what they are thinking and feeling.
- Body language can include (Bradberry, 2017):
  o Crossed arms and legs.
  o Smiles that crinkle the eyes.
  o Copying your body language.
  o Posture.
  o Eyes.
  o Raised eyebrows.
  o Exaggerated nodding.
  o Clenched jaw.
- Eye accessing cues can help determine which representational system is being accessed by the client.
- Types of preferred representational systems include visual, auditory, and kinesthetic.
- Behavior indicators of preferred representational systems include
  o Visual behavioral indicators:
- Neat and orderly.
- Observant.
- Appearance-oriented.
- More deliberate.
- Memorizes by picture.
  o Auditory behavioral indicators:
- Learns by listening.
- Very talkative.
- Uses a phonetic approach when spelling.
- Enjoys reading out loud.

- Talks better than they write.
  - o Kinesthetic behavioral indicators.
- Touches people and stands close.
- Moves a lot.
- Larger physical reaction.
- Early large muscle development.
- Learns through manipulation.
- Controlling people through a preferred representational system can be accomplished through applying NLP techniques and tools.

In the next chapter, you will learn about getting inside people's heads through the use of body language.

CHAPTER FIVE:

Getting Inside People's Heads Through Body Language

Reasons for Learning and Mastering Body Language Reading and Application

Since body language is a more accurate indicator of an individual's state of mind due to how thoughts and feelings communicate and express themselves more naturally through it, learning and mastering body language is a valuable skill for discerning other people's intentions and motivations. In other words, people's intentions and motivations become clearer when you understand the reasons behind their body language. Whether it is to leave an impression on your coworkers or communicate the need for affection, learning and mastering body language will help you get what you want out of life as you master the manifestations and forms of expression.

People also use body language to give other people their opinions and judgments, and learning and mastering body language could also be useful for this reason. Some career fields may require learning and mastering body language for judgment or assessment include psychology, law, and even education. The impression an individual leaves through their body language can have consequences, depending on the context. For instance, a psychological assessment can affect the medicine prescribed to a patient. Case in point, according to Radwan,

93% of the impressions people establish about you is surmised by body language, whereas only 7% of that impression is based on the words you use (2017). Even so, remember that how you communicate through words is always just as valuable as body language.

Gaining Advantage Through Body Language

Using body language advantageously can benefit yourself in many ways. One of those benefits comes with using it for attraction. An individual can attract a potential partner through using their body language; if done right and with the right amount of communication, the arrangement can eventually lead to love and affection. Some people may use body language to lead people on, making the other person assume that the former likes them, when in fact, they don't. This may be advantageous to the individual because that person can conceal their true feelings, intentions, and motivations better from any frenemies they have, as necessary and to keep personal boundaries.

Another advantage of using body language to your advantage is being able to induce specific states of mind. This is called the **reverse effect** because, when an individual moves their body or poses in a certain way, specific states of mind can materialize in them. For example, if you stand with your back straight and elevate your head a little, you may start to gain feelings of confidence, giving you stronger beliefs in your abilities. Another example of the reverse effect is when an individual smiles. Someone else's smile can trick your brain into happiness by initiating a chemical reaction that improves your mood, decreases stress and blood pressure, and may even increase your lifespan (Spector, 2018). As we've seen through these examples, it can be advantageous to use body language, as it can enhance both your subjective state of mind and wellbeing.

Most Useful Body Language to Interpret and Take Control

There are various types of body language of which we can interpret and take control to optimize our individual situations, depending on the context and reason. For example, if the reason is to garner more sales, then the salesperson's body language should reflect confidence when persuading the customer to buy. However, if their body language does not reflect this emotion, then they can take a class or go to a professional about body language, so they can learn how to appear and feel more confident and relaxed on the job.

The interpretation of body language is not an exact science, however, partially because various cultures may have assigned different meanings to body language. According to Zhi-Peng, gestures can be challenging to interpret because any slight variations can convey any number of completely different meanings (2014). For instance, American culture has assigned the OK sign (pressing thumb and forefinger together, other three fingers spread out) as approval, whereas in France, the same sign would suggest that the other person is "worthless" or "zero" (as indicated by the circle created between the two principal fingers). Another example of body language meaning different things is eye contact—in the United States and Canada, direct eye contact shows sincerity or interest, whereas the same eye cue in Japan is considered disrespectful (Zhi-Peng, 2014). Be that as it may, the same body language can also convey common meanings in terms of body movements, gestures, facial expressions, and eye movements.

Someone is Offended, Uneasy, Shy, or Defensive

A person's state of mind can also be revealed when they are offended, uneasy, shy, or defensive. More indicatively, the person feeling any of these emotions will usually cross their arms and possibly their legs too, if the situation is intense enough. If you notice another person is uncomfortable as a result of being in an unfamiliar environment, perhaps at a big gathering for work, that person will probably be folding the arms as a form of protection against that unfamiliar situation. This is why the posture is called the **defensive body language posture**, signaling one's uneasiness to those around them. It's almost as if the individual believes that by folding or crossing their arms and/or legs, they will supposedly be safer or protected from that environmental influence.

In addition, the defensive body language posture is also usually accompanied by additional facial expressions and specific body movements. Some of those facial expressions and body movements expressed during this time include recoil, a microaggression of anger, a clenched jaw, and pursed lips. For example, when an individual dislikes an uncomfortable situation or person, that individual will pull back or recoil. On the other hand, micro expressions of anger are also common when a person reacts defensively, in part because that individual's eyebrows will come down and their nose and top lip will come up, portraying disgust. As mentioned, another way to tell if a person is offended is when the person clenches their jaw tightly. In this defensive body movement, the person would have their jaw come forward and be possibly gritting their teeth, though you may not see it. Pursed lips are another indicator that an individual is uneasy and tense, usually done so the person can stop themselves from expressing vocally what they feel and believe.

However, the situation can be rectified or controlled when the individual takes responsibility for the offense. You can help them do this by asking them how they feel—this question can be accompanied by asking if they feel offended and how the situation can be rectified. This is useful to NLP because, if the NLP Practitioner can sense the other person's state of mind, that professional will have an easier time guiding that situation toward improvement. Once that is done and both parties feel comfortable, they can then continue the NLP session.

Someone is Evaluating or Thinking

When someone holds their chin in their hand, as if holding the weight of their thoughts and ideas, they are indicating that they are thinking or evaluating a situation. For example, I would often find myself doing this gesture when I write. In addition, someone using this body language to communicate is suggesting that they are listening to your ideas and thoughts while not only evaluating them, but also considering whether they are convincing enough. You would know if you have succeeded in getting through to someone if they nod their head while cupping their chin.

A thinker/evaluator's body language can also display whether their evaluation is positive or negative based on their use of gestures, such as smiling or clapping. However, there are other, less obvious positive cues that the other person may use, such as rubbing their eyebrow or adjusting their glasses—with the former, it's almost as if they were hoping to see the positive picture more clearly by moving their eyebrow hair out of the way (Parvez, 2015). I know I have adjusted my glasses plenty of times while evaluating something I view more positively than negatively.

There are also negative evaluation gestures that a person can use to signify a weak opinion of something. Some of the more obvious gestures pertaining to negative evaluation include closing eyes or looking away. These gestures will definitely let the other person know you are not quite in favor of the ideas they are presenting to you. Another gesture someone may employ is a little subtler: rubbing their nose. People may usually use this when they are angry, anxious, or self-conscious. It is also interesting to note that some people may be rubbing their nose to satisfy inflammation in that area brought upon by an increase in blood pressure when they lie—this phenomenon is known as the **Pinocchio Effect** (Parvez, 2015). This biological mechanism is efficient in lie detection, which is then useful in a variety of situations and careers associated with NLP practice.

Someone is Frustrated

Frustration can manifest outwardly in many ways through body language. It is easy to understand and interpret when the person does specific gestures, such as shaking their foot, tapping their hands in their lap, rubbing their face with their fingers, or even scratching themselves vigorously (Radwan, 2017). These frustrated movements can, in effect, release pent up energy within that person, especially when there is a situation that they cannot act upon. Still, the most obvious and widely accepted forms of frustration are when the person rubs the back of their neck or scratches the back of their head. Rubbing the back of one's neck while dealing with frustrating circumstances can help the person calm down because they are expanding that energy from its source.

We can also detect frustration through subtler body language, such as through someone's facial muscles, eyebrows, or lips. Slight movements in these areas are called **micro gestures**. For example, when I am feeling stressed or frustrated, my facial muscles may sometimes twitch. Other people may barely notice it; however, a professional trained in recognizing body language and cues may pick up on it. If someone is watching their friend—someone they probably know relatively intimately—they should be able to pick up those micro gestures much easier than if someone else were to because they can recognize their friend's behavior better. It is important to be able to detect micro gestures in your body language too, before trying to judge them in someone else's body language; for instance, a psychologist would be more effective if they are more aware of their own micro gestures prior to judging those of a client.

Someone is Anxious

Another form of body language that we can interpret easily is anxiety. When someone is anxious, they are usually expressing that feeling by fidgeting, usually in a number of different ways. Some of these fidgeting cues include sweating, fingernail biting, or constantly tapping one's fingers or heels on a table or on the ground. A personal example of mine would be that, whenever I have to wait at the doctor's office for an exam, I may fidget in my seat out of nerves. I may also move my left leg up and down quickly in an attempt to expend this nervous energy as I wait for the doctor to call my name.

In addition, expressing anxiety can affect various motor functions, such as walking or running, because that energy is causing one's body to become more rigid rather than relaxed. Originally, our ancestors would conceal themselves from predators by standing rigid and still, so they can avoid danger. It was as if their subconscious mind tightened up their bodies to avoid being recognized. Such instinct still appears similarly today. Oddly enough, it could be considered a form of ghosting, as the person tries to withdraw from observation. This anxious body language can be directed by an NLP Practitioner, with the professional trying to entice the person to calm down and perhaps even engage in some deep breathing exercises.

Someone is Bored

As we have seen, a person's body language can signal various states of mind, and this includes boredom. Boredom can be signaled by a person having droopy eyes, seeming inattentive, yawning, or fidgeting. As a personal example, when I get bored, I tend to feel tired, especially when I get stuck in a daily routine. The reasons for expressing boredom through body language include both a lack of interest and/or a readiness to take action. For example, when people drone on about subjects such as politics, it can put me to sleep because I have no interest in the topic. There are many reasons for boredom to occur.

The language of boredom is expressed in many ways, including tiredness, repetition, and distraction. For example, when an individual is bored, that person will distract themselves by engaging in other activities, such as looking at their cell phone. In addition, the individual trying to distract themselves as a result of boredom will usually avoid looking at the source of boredom, that being possibly a person or homework. Some distracting activities are repetitive, such as constantly tapping one's fingers. Last but not least, a person expressing boredom will sometimes look on blankly, in addition to having a slouched body. This posture could signal to a therapist or NLP Practitioner to switch it up or change the course of therapy.

Someone is Ready for the Next Step

Body language that indicates a person is ready to act can include pointing, tension, hooking, and movement. For instance, if one's body is pointed toward a person of interest—possibly the NLP Practitioner—then it is usually a sign that the former wants to take the next step in a sequence of events. In terms of tension, if a person is tense because they are doing something out of their comfort zone, their arms may grip onto something; for example, if you were at the dentist, you may be gripping the armrests on the chair while the dentist works on your teeth, completely ready to get out of that situation.

Hooking is another form of body language to indicate that the person is ready to take action. For this form, the person's hands hook slightly into their clothing, usually a waistband, and they would do this to show they are ready to move quickly if they need. Continuing with the subject of movement to demonstrate readiness, note that the beginning or first movement always lays the groundwork for further, successive movement. For example, I have a tendency to straighten the clothing under my coat before I go somewhere, like to a restaurant. The next movement I may do would usually be grabbing my purse on my way out the door.

Beyond the readiness language mentioned, there are also various reasons for why someone would be wanting to take action at that time. Some of these reasons include the person is leaving, ready to buy, continuing a conversation, or is ready to fight. If I am pointing in the direction of the door, my reason for doing so is because I want to leave or exit the situation. A person may be using readiness language when they are ready to buy a particular product, displaying the language to the salesperson when they point to that product. If my partner and I have an animated discussion, either one or both of us will be sending readiness signals to each other as we talk or continue the conversation. The final reason we will be mentioning here is during a fight when a person is readying their body to defend or attack. As a stubborn sibling, I would sometimes get into physical fights with my other siblings.

Using readiness language could be beneficial in many relationships, whether professional or personal, because such indicates to the other party that action needs to happen for that relationship to proceed in a positive direction. It would, therefore, be time to engage the individual with action if that person is ready.

Someone is Lying

Body language that reveals when somebody is lying usually involves shifts from that person's usual behavior. For example, if your friend usually meets your gaze when having a conversation, but that friend starts avoiding eye contact one day, then it could be an indicator that they are lying to you. When someone tells a lie, their amygdala—the part of the brain that processes emotions— becomes less responsive. This circumstance could escalate to the person becoming better at lying, so they may do it again successively. However, shifts in body language can still give them away. According to Jalili, movements of the body, expressions on their face, speech content, and tone of voice can all reveal a liar (2019).

One example of body language or behavior that implies a person is lying is movement involving hands. Hands that gesture after a conversation are telltale signs of a liar because, as the conversation is taking place, the liar's brain is too busy making up the lie and checking to see if you believe it. As a result, the hands may not gesture properly as they should during a conversation.

Another example of body language that a liar may use is squirming or fidgeting, as the person becomes increasingly nervous about getting caught. Nerves or nervous system changes can cause people to feel itchy or tingly, which provokes more fidgeting. This excessive body movement is not the norm for somebody telling the truth unless that person normally fidgets a lot.

A person may use facial expressions involving their eyes, mouth, or expressions when they lie. If the person lying during a conversation looks away a lot, it is because they are trying to think of what to make up next regarding the lie being told. On the other hand, if someone stares directly at you for way too long during a conversation, that could also suggest something is amiss. It is important to remember that the baseline behavior for the individual is usually different from when the person tells a lie. Mouth or lip movements also impart a lie when the person's lips roll back, which is a suggestion that they are holding back facts (Jalili, 2019). The individual's complexion may also change if they are telling a lie. It could go one of two ways—they become as white as a ghost, or flushed. Body language can be quite telling, especially during interrogations.

Speech content may also change when a person lies. For example, when someone says "I want to be honest with you," implies they felt the need to add an emphasis on their honesty to make up for a potential lie. Another example of speech changing during a lie is when the liar is looking for the words to make up the lie. In this case, while the person is thinking of the next word to use, they may use filler words such as "um" or "uh" numerous times during their lie. In addition, the person's tone of voice may become higher pitched, indicating they are stressed or nervous when telling the lie. This stress causes the vocal cords to become rigid as they tighten. As we've seen here, the act of lying clearly has its own body language, which is helpful in psychology as well as law.

Micro Expressions

Micro expressions are also a form of body language that can indicate various states of mind within an individual and whether that person is lying. Some universal micro expressions include that of fear, happiness, disgust, surprise, sadness, anger, and contempt. A micro expression is hard to fake because they are involuntary expressions on the face that occur when a particular emotion is felt (Markowitz, 2013). For instance, when a person is genuinely surprised, they may raise their eyebrows with their skin stretching under the eyebrow, have wrinkles on their forehead appear, open their eyes wide, and drop their jaw.

Such micro expressions on the face during an emotional experience do not last a very long time: about 1/15 to 1/25 of a second (Babich, 2016). Truth speakers and liars will display different forms of micro expressions because those expressions are involuntary, making them more accurate indicators of genuine thought. An NLP Practitioner can use their analysis of their client's micro expressions to gauge the latter's true state of mind and determine the next course of action pertaining to the client's life and the NLP session. In addition, the NLP Practitioner can reprogram the individual to go in the direction of a more beneficial outcome, given the authenticity of micro expressions, even when the client is lying about how they truly feel.

Talk to the Hand: Telltale Handshakes and Gestures

Another form of body language that can be interpreted and even controlled are handshakes and gestures. This form of hand-body language can be very telling about a person because the positions of their hands can display their intentions. For example, if a person is sociable, their handshake will probably be firmer than someone who is more introverted, whose handshake would probably be looser. In addition, a handshake can also be employed to impart dominance, shown if the person initiates the handshake, then uses their hand to guide or otherwise control yours (Muoio, 2014). Other forms of handshakes include the finger-crushing shake, the two-hander shake, the sweaty shake, the finger shake, and the no cup shake. The two-hander is arguably the most interesting handshake because it is usually used to reveal sincerity, honesty, and even intimacy, especially when the handshake is higher up than usual. However, this handshake can still be misleading, for example, when political leaders want to front friendship to outsiders, they may cup the other person's hand in a desire to take control!

Hand-body language also includes hand gestures, like showing open palms, pointing at somebody, steeping their fingers in front of one's face, standing with hands behind one's back, and clenching hands (Muoio, 2014). When someone shows open palms, this can suggest openness—unless the palms are down, instead suggesting authority. Pointing can suggest aggressiveness, whereas steeping your fingers in front of your face imparts confidence. You would often see people standing with their hands behind their back in the military when standing "at ease;" it would generally be used to show the opposite of superiority and power, along with respect to those who are in power. Be that as it may, clenching one's hands indicates frustration.

Handshakes become more memorable when they are done properly, depending on the context. The context could be a business meeting or a social gathering, and handshakes can leave quite a lasting impression during these events. In terms of neuroscience, a handshake can promote a positive atmosphere, full of good intentions and motivations. A confident handshake can suggest communication on a deeper level, reduced negative associations, and increased personal interest (Lee, 2020). It is evident that a good handshake can set the stage for further positive communications and interactions.

It's important to note that hand gestures can also convey meaning. For instance, shoving your hands in your pockets will project a reluctance to talk, whereas open palms can suggest sincerity. In addition, a downward-facing palm can suggest authority and power, whereas a closed hand with the finger pointed can signal an attempt to get someone to submit. For example, when your parents give you a directive, they

58

may use a closed hand with a pointed finger to convince you effectively to submit to their authority. Other hand gestures include the precision thumbs, gripping fingertips, fist thrusting, and hand chopping. As we've discovered, hand gestures can tell you a lot about a person and their intentions.

Persuasive Body Language

Persuasive body language can project confidence in all sorts of situations, from professional to personal. Some body language gestures that reflect self-confidence include hands in front of stomach, fingertips touching, and using a power pose. For example, I notice the meteorologist I watch on television in the mornings always places his hands with the fingertips touching in front of his stomach, as he gives the weather report for the day. He appears to be very confident, even when he slips on his words. Other body language confidence gestures include (Radwan, 2017):

- Upright posture.
- Walking with wide steps.
- Doesn't panic.
- No fidgeting.
- Fewer speech mistakes.
- Proper eye contact.
- No closed gestures.
- Not looking to others for what to do regarding future actions.

It is important to be able to be able to read these body language signals in yourself and others because you will not only feel more confident and attractive, but the signals themselves will also convince people to like you more. For example, if my partner walks with wide steps, it may imply that they have no fear when encountering unfamiliar situations. In addition, many people find confidence to be sexy.

Body language signals are also valuable to professionals and businesses alike, especially when the salesperson is trying to persuade a prospect into buying their product and/or service. Some of these readable body signals come from the eyes, face, hands, arms, and feet. For example, when a potential customer is staring at the product you're trying to sell, it may be a good time to ask if they have any questions about it. If the customer smiles and nods at the same time, your presentation of the product was likely successful and you are probably good to go.

In addition, hands and arms can also communicate impatience, generally when the person drums their fingers (Wood, n.d.). Feet are also good to analyze, as they can signal whether the prospect is open or closed off to the salesperson, depending on the direction in which they are pointed. If the feet are pointed toward the salesperson, then they are open to the salesperson's ideas, whereas when the opposite occurs, they are probably unappreciative of the salesperson's advice. Body language signals such as these can tell the salesperson a lot about the customer's reaction to themselves and their product, so it is critical to learn as much about the various body signals as soon as possible.

Persuasion and Influence in NLP

Body language becomes more influential and persuasive when a person can mirror or match that of another person. For example, during an NLP session between a client and the NLP Practitioner, reading the other's body language and signals can become like a game. If the client smiles, so would the NLP Practitioner because doing so creates rapport and trust when people see you are similar to them. This NLP rapport can then be guided and manipulated in the direction the NLP Practitioner wants it to go as they lead the client with their intentional body signals.

Persuasion and influence in NLP practice by means of NLP techniques and tools becomes possible when using one NLP technique in particular—**framing**. Framing is when the NLP Practitioner sets up the context of the situation by repeating back to the individual their original context. They would usually do this by restating it to indicate their own similarity to the person, thus building rapport. After all, the best words to hear are ones you just said! NLP framing is just one of the many NLP techniques and tools that can be quite influential and persuasive when done correctly.

If it is done correctly, it is possible to change a person's subjective state of mind by NLP framing. The NLP Practitioner would frame by controlling the context through the use of one's own subjective state, mirror neurons, language, and intention (Snyder, 2019). All these variables help to convince the client to anchor to the NLP Practitioner, thus building rapport and trust. Once the client trusts the NLP Practitioner, the client will use language to amplify their original state with trigger words. These trigger words can then be used by the NLP Practitioner to lead the client into further discussion by opening up a memory with values, associations, and emotional **hot buttons**. The hot buttons animate the client emotionally and can produce more feelings that change the client's perceptual filters. This is when the client will start to perceive the NLP Practitioner by the picture that the former just created of themselves. As you can see, NLP framing can be a very powerful tool of control, manipulation, and persuasion.

Chapter Summary

In this chapter, you have learned why you should learn and master body language. In addition, you have learned how to gain an advantage through the use of body language, while also understanding its most important forms, so you can interpret and take control of them. It is also important to remember what we went over about micro expressions, handshakes, gestures because understanding them better can help you influence and persuade others much easier. Furthermore, mirroring is another influential and persuasive technique to build rapport, especially when framing. To refresh your memory, the following are some of the key points from this chapter:

- Non-verbal body language can be an accurate indicator of a person's communication.
- You can gain an advantage in any situation by using persuasive body language.
- Although the general use of body language is universal, various cultures may interpret forms of it in different ways.
- Body language can indicate strong feelings.
- Involuntary expression of micro expressions can be useful to the practice of NLP because the NLP Practitioner can then gauge the client's true state of mind.
- Handshakes and gestures can reveal the client's true state of mind.
- Persuasive body language projects confidence in all sorts of situations, from professional to personal.
- Some forms of persuasive body language include (Radwan, 2017):
  o Upright posture.
  o Walking with wide steps.
  o Doesn't panic.
  o No fidgeting.
  o Fewer speech mistakes.
  o Proper eye contact.
  o No closed gestures.
  o Not looking to others for what to do regarding actions.
- Body language becomes more influential and persuasive when it can be mirrored or matched to fit the other person's body language, thus possibly influencing them to take action.
- NLP framing is a powerful NLP tool that an NLP Practitioner can use to control, manipulate, and persuade a client.

In the next chapter, you will learn all about NLP frame control.

CHAPTER SIX:

Control the Frame, Control the Game

NLP Framing Interpreted

NLP framing can be defined as the boundaries encapsulating an event or experience. In other words, a **frame** in NLP terminology is a person's mental template that filters or colors their everyday perceptions, influencing their behaviors and interactions (Catherine, 2014). In NLP framing, the person's mental template can be changed, altering how they see and experience reality; reality would change as the person experiences it if an NLP Practitioner "framed" the person.

Brain's Response to NLP Framing

NLP framing affects the brain through the restructuring of limbic system links between the amygdala and the hippocampus. The **amygdala** is in charge of managing your emotions, while the **hippocampus** produces and stores your most relevant memories. More specifically, the **prefrontal cortex** and the **thalamus** interact with the hippocampus, amygdala, and the rest of the limbic system to fish out the memory that is most appropriate for the attempt at NLP framing.

NLP Framing Edits an Emotional Response

Thus, NLP framing edits the emotional response to that specific memory by increasing or decreasing the emotions associated with that memory. For example, negative framing can decrease the person's emotions by assisting them with detaching themselves from that memory. This negative framing would accomplish this task through subduing or inhibiting any links between the emotions and that memory. On the other hand, positive framing tries to amplify an otherwise normal memory into a more powerful one by using the person's imagination and senses, putting in extra focus toward increasing its emotional impact.

NLP Framing Based on Intentions

NLP framing is based on intentions. More specifically, NLP framing is based on the intentions of the NLP Practitioner and the client as they interact during an NLP session, based on the reasons for having the session in the first place. For example, if the client wished to have the session because they wanted to reframe an experience they had as more positive, then the intentions of the NLP Practitioner would probably be to increase any positive associations and feelings they have toward that event or memory. The reasons for improving the client's subjective state of mind in reference to the event or memory would be that the client benefits emotionally, psychologically, and maybe even physically.

Categories of Intentions in NLP Framing

There are also categories of intentions when it comes to NLP framing. Some of those categories include subconscious intentions, conscious intentions, preset intentions, evolving intentions, and conditional intentions. **Subconscious intentions** are hidden or suppressed from conscious awareness, whereas **conscious intentions** are intentions we pay close attention to, and would usually be the kind that occupy our daily thoughts. For example, you may be "in the zone" while working on a task and may not even be aware of it, given subconscious intentions; however, you are conscious about the *purpose* for the task. **Preset intentions** usually involve plans, whereas **evolving intentions** happen in the moment. **Conditional intentions**, interestingly enough, are useful if the conditions for it are met. As we've seen, there are various competing intentions in life and in NLP practice.

Setting Strong Frames in NLP

Setting strong frames in NLP is sometimes necessary to accomplish the overall objective. This is because there are many variables that can affect the strength of the frame's intentions, such as time, flexibility, and knowledge. For instance, a short-term time frame can be strong, like getting groceries from the store, whereas a long-term time frame, like paying down debt, can be weaker. In addition, flexibility plays a role because, if you can work within subframes to accomplish the objective of the main frame, then the chances of success become higher than if you remained inflexible. Knowledge also plays a key role because, the more knowledge the individual has, the more likely they can accomplish the overall objective. Strong frames require strong intentions as well, even if there are many frame strength variables along the way.

Knowing What NLP Frame to Adopt

Figuring out which NLP frame to adopt for the individual context is key because the frame can affect the client, direction, goals, and overall outcome of the NLP session. If the NLP Practitioner is aware of the individual they are trying to persuade, then it will be easier to choose the right frame. Such personal variables include who the individual's identity, their motivations, chosen form of expression, micro expressions, values, and what they really want (Snyder, 2019). Once this knowledge is obtained, then it becomes easier to convince the person to do what you want. Knowing what frame to adopt can also be determined by answering the following questions:

65

- What does this person need to be for them to take the actions I want?
- What subjective states of mind does the person have to be in to want to take those actions?
- What's in it for the person?
- What is the outcome?

If the correct frame is chosen for that individual, the person will become more than likely to open up, which will ultimately help both the NLP Practitioner and the client. More specifically, the correct frame will help the NLP Practitioner elicit the information the professional needs to move the NLP therapy session in the direction it needs to go, and the client will benefit from the outcome.

Reasons for Creating a Strong Frame in NLP

To create a strong frame, the NLP Practitioner will have to adhere to a few prerequisites. One such requirement is a strong intention, which is necessary to ascertain the will of the client and see the task through to its fulfillment. Another requirement for a strong frame is flexibility, due to there sometimes being various subframes within the main frame. If the NLP Practitioner isn't flexible, then it will become more challenging to accomplish the main objective of the NLP therapy session. The next requirement for a strong frame is that the client and NLP Practitioner would need to put it to the test to determine its tolerance and strength of survival. For instance, if my goal is to lose weight, then I have to take action repeatedly to make that happen, especially if I am tempted to fall off the horse by binging out at a buffet. Strong frames also require the individual not to shift and redefine the frame because doing so will only make them lose sight of the original goal. In short, a person has to hold firm to accomplish the objectives and goals of the frame.

NLP Frame Strengthening Exercises

Sometimes NLP frames need to be strengthened to become and remain strong. To do this task, the person can follow a few frame strengthening exercises. Some of those exercises include:

- Avoid cursing or using strong swear words.
- Adhere to a shopping list.
- Stick to a regular sleep schedule.
- Work out everyday.
- Have concrete life goals.
- Socialize, but keep score.
- Incline people to smile.
- Take an acting class.
- Engage in Tai Chi in public.
- Keep score of the intentions set before every conversation.

The reasons for some of these frame strengthening exercises include learning how to control oneself by sticking to something like a shopping list, a regular sleep schedule, and the like. In addition, having well-defined, concrete life goals can give the individual something to work toward. Socializing helps develop stronger frame control as the person interacts with more people, while inclining people to smile will pull others in emotionally. It is also suggested to take acting classes for stronger frame control because doing so will teach the person to "act" well while employing strong frame control. Engaging in exercises such as Tai Chi in a public space can also help the individual learn to no longer care about what others are thinking and the fact that others are watching them. Lastly, keeping score on conversational intentions will improve frame control because the person would be practicing following through on those intentions.

7 NLP Frames and How to Apply Them

There is a variety of NLP Frames in NLP practice, and some of those NLP frames are the Outcome Frame, the Ecology Frame, the As If Frame, the Backtrack Frame, the Relevancy Frame, the Contrast Frame, and the Open Frame. The **Outcome Frame**, more defined, is an exercise that will help you discover what people want, then learn the resources to acquire their wants. It is applied by simply asking the individual what they want. Another frame is the **Ecology Frame**, which is defined as the impact of an action or event on the bigger systems in which we take part, such as family, community, and even the entire planet. The Ecology Frame is applied by asking about the integrity of the desired action and how that affects the integrity of others and their respective systems.

On the other hand, the **As If Frame** implies that a person should fake it until they make it, allowing for the exploration of possibilities and innovative problem solving if the situation were different. Beyond that, the **Backtrack Frame** is defined as returning to a point of reference to clarify the information, so the person can move forward and realign the direction of the communication and interaction. It is applied by restating what was said by using the other individual's keywords, which checks if there is understanding and agreement.

Then there is the **Relevancy Frame**, which keeps the discussion pertinent by asking "how is that relevant to the outcome or agenda of this discussion?" The **Contrast Frame** is defined as comparing and contrasting options and alternatives to show that action needs to be taken now. This frame is applied by contrasting the present situation with the desired outcome, which helps highlight which action should be taken. Finally, the **Open Frame** is completely non-scripted, allowing the individual to discuss and express whatever it is they feel like talking about at that specific moment. As we can see, these frames can be quite useful and can be applied to a variety of contexts to help the recipient toward the desired outcome.

Reframing in NLP

Reframing the original NLP frame can be beneficial in certain circumstances—when the original NLP frame no longer applies to the current context, it must be restructured and adapted to be viable again to the individual and the situation. According to Hall, **reframing** is defined as shifting our thoughts with a different perspective resulting from reclassifying and redefining the frame-of-reference into a different classification or category (2010). In effect, reframing allows us to be more creative, as it supplies a new reference structure from which to view things. This, in turn, can change our experiences, thoughts, and interactions, among other things.

Reframing can be accomplished in a few different ways, including de-framing, pre-framing, post-framing, counter-framing, outframing, and metaphorical framing. **De-framing** is when we pull the meaning apart, whereas **pre-framing** is when the idea of action is reclassified. In addition, **post-framing** is when a point of view is established beforehand by structuring a frame ahead of time. Post-framing is creating new points of view from a future reference point, so that, when the person refers to a previous action, a different meaning would materialize. Furthermore, **counter-framing** requires counter examples to be provided to the person and/or context. **Outframing** is defined as creating a new frame about the idea by stepping aside from a meaning, thus allowing the other frame into existence. Last but not least, **metaphorical framing** is when a story or a metaphor is used to frame things in a similar situation. Reframing allows the individual to adapt creatively to change while the person's mental versatility frames and reframes their subjective experiences.

Using Frame Control to Influence People

Frame control can be used to persuade people by demonstrating behavior consistency through congruence in facial gestures, tone of voice, and body language, ultimately pulling people into going along with you (Your Charisma Coach, 2020). For example, if I listen consistently to what my partner has to say by leaning in and looking them directly in the eyes, they will be more likely to go along with my ideas or suggestions when I have something to say. In short, my consistent behavior is what will keep my partner's interest, and he will hopefully follow my lead. Frame control is influential because it sets social expectations that can make a powerful impression on the person, as long as you don't change your behavior toward them. Frame control sets the stage for further actions and reactions once you have defined it.

The Russell Brand Method and Exploiting Other People's Words and Weaknesses

One interesting frame control strategy is the Russell Brand Method. The **Russell Brand Method** of frame control includes a strong belief system, confident body language, clear state of mind in which emotions don't overwhelm, and capability to exploit another individual's words. More explicitly, a strong belief system with a powerful vision will support the arguments of the individual, given continual practice of that belief system. Secondly, confident body language also influences frame control, displayed by baring one's chest, practicing a commanding tone of voice, walking like a CEO, and being aware of one's gestures and body language postures (Iliopoulos, 2015). In addition, a clear state of mind in which emotions don't overwhelm is also important because it allows the individual to control the frame in comparison to losing it.

Still, the capacity to exploit others' individual words is also a powerful aid in the Russell Brand Method because doing so allows the person to turn it back around onto the messenger. For example, if the person is unaffected by other peoples' attempts to harass them, it is suggesting a calmer presence, thus giving the individual time to assess the words used against them. The Russell Brand Method of frame control is effective in exploiting people's words and weaknesses because most people react to the situation instead of taking action themselves.

Taking Back Control of Your Own Mind in Frame Wars

Taking back control of your own mind in frame wars is necessary to be able to manipulate the situation back in your favor. This can be done by challenging the unobserved and by creating a new discussion (Basu, 2016). Challenging the unobserved will allow the individual to make the other party talk about the bigger perspective, thus giving the former the chance to divert from the actual discussion. Furthermore, this act interrupts the other party and their thinking. In addition, asking questions can create another discussion in which the person can lead the other party away from their frame and mindset. In other words, the second part of taking back control of your own mind in frame wars is to create a new discussion, as doing so pulls the other party out of their own frame and gets them to consider and talk about other relevant frames. This method is useful for leading a conversation in their favor.

Chapter Summary

In this chapter, you have learned about various aspects of NLP frame control. You have learned about what framing is, as well as how to set a strong frame. You have also learned about the seven NLP frames and how to apply them, while considering the art of reframing itself. Also, critical to note is the use of frame control to influence people; for example, the Russell Brand Method. Last but not least, you have learned how to take back control of your own mind in frame wars. To refresh your memory, here are the key points of this chapter:

- A frame is a person's mental template that filters their everyday perceptions, which would then influence the person's behaviors and interactions (Catherine, 2014).
- NLP framing affects the brain through restructuring limbic system links between the amygdala and the hippocampus.
- NLP framing edits the emotional response to a specific memory by increasing or decreasing the emotions associated with the memory.

- NLP framing is based on intentions.
- NLP framing has the following categories of intentions:
  o Subconscious intentions.
  o Conscious intentions.
  o Preset intentions.
  o Evolving intentions.
  o Conditional intentions.
- Setting strong frames is sometimes necessary to accomplish the overall objective.
- Knowing which frame to adopt for the individual context is key, and can be determined by asking:
  o What does this person need to be for them to take the actions I want?
  o What subjective states of mind does the person have to be in to want to take those actions?
  o What's in it for the person?
  o What is the outcome?
- Frame strengthening exercises are sometimes necessary to strengthen the frame. Some exercises include the following:
  o Avoid cursing or using strong swear words.
  o Adhere to a shopping list.
  o Stick to a regular sleep schedule.
  o Work out everyday.
  o Have concrete life goals.
  o Socialize but keep score.
  o Incline people to smile.
  o Take an acting class.
  o Engage in Tai Chi in public.
  o Keep score of the intentions set before every conversation.
- There is a variety of NLP frames, some of which include:
  o Outcome Frame.
  o Ecology Frame.
  o As If Frame.
  o Backtrack Frame.
  o Relevancy Frame.

- o Contrast Frame.
- o Open Frame.
- Reframing is shifting our thoughts to a different perspective resulting from reclassifying and redefining the frame-of-reference into a different classification or category (Hall, 2010).
- Frame control can persuade people by demonstrating behavior consistency through congruence in facial gestures, tone of voice, and body language, ultimately pulling people into going along with you (Your Charisma Coach, 2020).
- The Russell Brand Method of frame control includes a strong belief system, confident body language, clear state of mind in which emotions don't overwhelm, and the capability to exploit another individual's words.
- Taking back control of your own mind is done by challenging the unobserved and creating a new discussion.

In the next chapter, you will learn all about hypnosis and NLP Duo.

CHAPTER SEVEN:

Hypnosis and NLP's Potency

How Hypnosis and NLP Work Together

Hypnosis and NLP work together by influencing the mind and behaviors of an individual through their subconscious and conscience in similar ways. Since the subconscious can influence our thoughts, behaviors, actions, and vice versa, programming or restructuring the mind through hypnosis and NLP becomes quite effective. Both NLP and hypnosis use body language and tone of voice to influence the individual's subconscious, with the goal to put the individual in a more suggestive state. Within this state, the hypnotist or NLP Practitioner will have an easier time getting the person to follow the former's wishes. In addition, the effectiveness of NLP increases if the individual is hypnotized, as they become more open to influence, suggestion, and guidance. Similarly, if the individual is being reprogrammed through NLP, then their subconscious also acquires new ways of thinking and feeling about everyday experiences. Interesting to note is that while NLP programs the mind to discipline the subconscious to respond more efficiently to daily events, hypnotism uses the person's subconscious to influence their mind with a similar effect. In short, NLP influences the conscious mind to control the subconscious, whereas hypnotism influences the subconscious to then affect the conscious part of our brains. Combining these two practices is an effective method for improving an individual's life.

Rules of Hypnosis

Although NLP and hypnosis are very similar in their respective methods and outcomes, hypnosis has more free reign to influence the mind, given it is less scripted in its application and practice. Hypnosis has fewer presuppositions characterizing its practice, which allows it to have more leeway for free play. Even so, hypnosis has some important rules to help with its effectiveness. According to Casale, those rules are (2012):

- Don't hypnotize an individual who has epilepsy, a mental condition, or is otherwise disturbed.
- Don't try to construct subconscious changes.
- Leave out the theatrics and do not trick the individual.
- Avoid unexpected responses that can cause the individual to panic due to unexpected environmental changes. It is important to watch for this because there will be an increased environmental sensitivity on the individual's part.
- Ensure the individual is free from any induced beliefs when taking the person out of the trance.
- Be sure to take your time in a safe and controlled environment.
- Treat hypnotism as a relaxation tool, not an entertainment gimmick.

These rules for hypnosis practice are necessary for various reasons. One of those reasons is to treat the inductee ethically and with the utmost respect and consideration; treat them the same as you would hope another hypnotist or NLP Practitioner would to you. Another reason for the rules of hypnosis is to ensure that all parties involved are safe and sound before, during, and after the session. This assurance is necessary to prevent any mistreatment toward the individual, as well as any potential abuse of practice; otherwise, less desirable outcomes may occur. The rules of hypnosis help structure and guide its application into more ethically sound outcomes and benefits.

Setting, Priming, and Inducing Hypnosis

In addition to the rules of hypnosis, hypnosis is also distinguished by the setting, priming, and inducing of the inductee by the hypnotist. This is necessary to get the individual in the right frame of mind to undergo hypnosis. To initiate the hypnosis session, the **setting** itself must be ripe for relaxation, which is done by ensuring the inductee is in a comfortable, relaxed, and usually inclined position, so they can become more calm and peaceful. Hypnotists will often make use of a comfortable couch, for example. In addition, it is critical that the hypnotist make sure there are no unexpected interruptions, like a sudden knock on the door, because this could interfere with the hypnosis and even bring the inductee out of their state too quickly, thus affecting the person subconsciously. Most importantly, the inductee needs to trust their hypnotist because, otherwise, the attempt will be less successful, given the inductee will be less confident that their hypnotist can effectively do the deed.

Also important to the practice of hypnosis is priming the person before the start of the session. More specifically, **priming** is the act of making something ready for action. In hypnosis, this is done by confusing the person, making them more suggestible while their prefrontal cortex becomes too busy trying to understand the confusion (Casale, 2012). It is akin to confusing a telemarketer purposefully to distract them from trying to sell you something you don't really need. For example, I could use bad grammar to throw off a person or even ask them a nonsensical question. Doing so will shock the person to the point where they may become even more suggestible, given the brain won't be as able to filter out the confusing message or suggestion with proper reason.

Once the stage has been set and the individual primed, it is time to induce hypnosis. This is done by instructing the inductee to relax progressively, deeper and deeper until their entire body is in a state of total relaxation. For example, the hypnotist could count backwards from ten to zero, with the goal to increase the sense of calm and tranquility within the individual. More specifically, the hypnotist will employ visualization and imagery by asking the client to imagine relaxing in a specific setting, as the hypnotist calmly counts backwards.

Inducing hypnosis requires the hypnotist to use a calm voice while expressing positive words and sentence structure because, otherwise, the intended meaning of the message may get muddled. It is all about the individual and their subjective state of mind and experience, so if they become uncomfortable for any reason, it becomes time to end the session by waking the person up carefully from the hypnosis.

Using Hypnosis and Magic Suggestive Language

Using hypnosis requires the power of suggestion through language. As we've seen, language can be influential, and we will learn that it is not only in *what* is said, but in *how* it is said. In other words, how the intended meaning is framed and characterized can influence how the recipient receives that message. For example, if I use directives instead of suggestions to convince someone to act, there will be less freedom of interpretation because the directive is more specific. Directing someone to clean their room is more specific than if I indirectly suggested it through ambiguous language that left room for interpretation, such as saying "Just do it." On the other hand, suggesting a course of action through non-specific language can be more influential and powerful because it leaves room for personalizing the intended meaning, given there is more room for that interpretation.

As was just mentioned, the magic of suggestive language is that it leaves plenty of room for interpretation with its purposeful vagueness. For example, Nike's slogan "Just Do It" allows the individual to take those words at face value and consciously. Along with this, the slogan also allows the person to develop a meaning unconsciously and specific to their current situation and context at that time (Evolution Development, n.d.). Similarly, television advertisements are known for being influential and suggestive with their vague language used to convince a person to buy their product or service.

In conclusion, vague language can be more suggestive and influential because it targets a person's subconscious, which is helpful in hypnosis because it allows the hypnotist to plant suggestions in the inductee's mind. With hypnosis, language is specifically vague but purposefully influential, with action verbs and other words used suggestively.

Milton Model Overview

Also using suggestive language is the **Milton Model**, which originated from the hypnotherapist Milton H. Erickson. Erickson utilized language effectively in his practice to achieve results faster than that used in traditional therapy. By requiring ambiguous yet influential language patterns in its practice, the Milton Model helps the client deduce their own meaning from the communication, then apply it to their experience of reality. This personalized interpretation can then be useful to the client's goals because it guides the action needed by the client to accomplish therapeutic results and outcomes. In short, the use of the Milton Model in therapy, hypnosis, or NLP is an effective tool to elicit action from the individual.

Dangers of Hypnosis

Speaking of manipulation and control, the dangers of hypnosis are very real. This is because some hypnotists do not have positive intentions, while others simply lack knowledge, which ends up causing unintended harm to the recipient. According to Tyrrell, the dark side to hypnosis that ethical hypnotists need to be aware of includes the following (2015):

- Taking away the inductee's volition.
- Questionable intentions of the hypnotist.
- Constructing false memories.
- Causing hallucinations.

- Unwanted telepathy.
- Hurting the individual's "essence" or character.

The risks and dangers associated with hypnosis warrant that the highest ethics and moral standards would have to be applied to avoid harming the individual psychologically, emotionally, and even physically as a result. Such harm may not only distress the individual, but also leave a lasting mark on their subconscious, affecting their everyday life detrimentally. If the hypnotist or hypnotherapist doesn't possess integrity and compassion, then the inductee might suffer from direct effects toward their own life, such as loss of family, work, or mental health. Therefore, it is important to practice hypnosis ethically, so you can avoid negative consequences for everyone involved.

Resisting Hypnosis

On that note, sometimes it is necessary to build resistance to hypnosis when it is used covertly on you and without your permission. For example, consumerism involves the use of pervasive hypnotic advertisements layered with subliminal messaging—without your permission—to get you to spend your hard-earned money on a specific product or service. Knowing how to defend yourself before such a situation occurs is the best defense you have that can help you resist hypnosis temptation. Some of the best defenses to help you counteract and resist the powerful effects of hypnosis include (David, 2010):

- Knowledge and awareness of the self and psychology manipulation.
- Restating the hypnotist's thoughts for clarity.
- Refusing to give out any information about yourself.
- Putting off decisions until the experience is over.
- Not abandoning outside interests or contacts.
- Avoiding being around people who amplify guilt.
- Having at least one critical friend who is not afraid to doubt the veracity of any facts presented to you or them.

- Seeking information before joining a group.

It is also important to safeguard and protect your personal boundaries; otherwise, the hypnotists unethically engaging in covert hypnotism could be able to manipulate your feelings, thoughts, and behaviors once they get past your defenses. To avoid this, enforce your personal boundaries like a protective shield around your person in any way you can. That way, nothing sketchy or questionable can affect your integrity as an individual. Important to note is that some of these resistance techniques take practice to be effective against the more covert hypnotists.

Ways Hypnotists Break Resistance

On the other hand, there are ways hypnotists can break the recipient's resistance to their hypnotizing attempts. For example, the hypnotist can isolate the individual from familiar surroundings, such as family and friends. Doing so helps break that individual's resistance, as they get placed in unfamiliar territory, which then makes them more susceptible to external influences. Some other ways hypnotists break resistance include (David, 2010):

- Giving the person unconditional acceptance from a deceivingly friendly group of people.
- Isolating the individual from conflicting ideas.
- A false authority figure, seemingly having special knowledge that others look to for advice.
- A false philosophy that appears to have all the answers to your questions.
- Overwhelming the person with activities that result in less autonomy of thought or action.
- Providing a false sense of "Us" versus "Them."
- Using covert hypnotic techniques.

However, resisting the hypnotists' attempts to brainwash the individual is possible if the latter is knowledgeable about the practice beforehand. Knowledge is *key!* Otherwise, if you don't know what can hurt you, you might end up becoming a tool or pawn for the hypnotists' benefits and goals. In this instance, ignorance does not equate to bliss and, unfortunately, there is a lot more information known for breaking down resistance than there is to build it up. More research is needed to protect the common individual from undue influence, control, and manipulative forces.

Covert Hypnosis Trance Signs

Speaking of manipulative forces, covert hypnosis includes many signs that the unknowing individual is either going, or already is, in a trance. For example, dilation of the pupils suggests the trance is beginning to take effect, as it displays relaxation in the individual's gaze. It is important to know these signs because otherwise the individual can get pulled something they might regret later via hypnosis. Some more trance signs of covert hypnosis include (Mask, 2020):

- Changes in pulse.
- Changes in breathing patterns.
- Facial features relaxing.
- Absorbed attention.
- Changes in the blink reflex.
- Eyelids get heavier.
- Person becomes motionless.
- Involuntary twitches of muscles.

Knowing the trance signs of covert hypnosis can help protect you and help you recognize if and when you are entering into a trance. Any individual who knows and can recognize these physical trance signs will be better equipped to resist unethical hypnosis practices. In addition, the individual will gain more control over their own reactions to the hypnosis attempt and respond appropriately by snapping out of it in time before something potentially detrimental happens. It is important to remember that the goals and outcomes of hypnosis and NLP should be constructive and beneficial to the individual, and not destructive.

Chapter Summary

In this chapter, you have learned about how hypnosis and NLP can work together to influence the mind, while also studying how hypnosis can use suggestive language to influence a person's subconscious. We have gone over the dangers of hypnosis and why it is sometimes vital to resist the attempt of the hypnotist if they are practicing an unethical covert hypnosis. Beyond that, you have also been educated about various ways hypnotists can break a person's resistance. It is also important to be aware of the trance signs of covert hypnosis to protect ourselves from undue influence. To refresh your memory, here are the key points of this chapter:

- Hypnosis and NLP work together by influencing the mind and behaviors of the individual through the subconscious and the conscience.
- The rules of hypnosis are to treat and influence the individual into the desired outcome ethically.
- Setting, priming, and inducing hypnosis is critical to the goals and outcome(s) of hypnosis.
- Vague language can be more suggestive and influential because it targets the individual's subconscious.
- The Milton Model was created to manufacture agreement in the individual by employing ambiguous yet influential language patterns.
- The risks and dangers associated with hypnosis warrant the highest ethics and moral standards to avoid harming the individual psychologically, emotionally, and even physically as a result.

- Building resistance to hypnosis is necessary when it is used covertly and without your permission.
- Some ways to counteract and resist hypnosis include (David, 2010):
  o Knowledge and awareness of self and psychological manipulation.
  o Restating the hypnotist's thoughts for clarity.
  o Refusing to give out any information about yourself.
  o Putting off decisions until the experience is over.
  o Not abandoning outside interests or contacts.
  o Avoiding being around people who amplify guilt.
  o Having at least one critical friend who is not afraid to doubt the veracity of the facts presented to either you or them.
  o Seeking information before joining the group.
- Equally important is knowing how hypnotists can break resistance, as it can help the individual avoid becoming a tool for any unstated agendas.
- Ways hypnotists break resistance include (David, 2010):
  o Giving the person unconditional acceptance from a deceivingly friendly group of people.
  o Isolating the individual from conflicting ideas.
  o A false authority figure who seems to have special knowledge that others look to for advice.
  o A false philosophy that appears to have all the answers to your questions.
  o Overwhelming the person with activities, which results in less autonomy of thought or action.
  o Providing a false sense of "Us" versus "Them."
  o Using covert hypnotic techniques.
- Knowing the trance signs of covert hypnosis can help the individual from becoming influenced unethically into doing or participating in something shady.
- Trance signs of covert hypnosis include (Mask, 2020):
  o Dilation of pupils.
  o Changes in pulse.

- o Changes in breathing patterns.
- o Facial features relaxing.
- o Absorbed attention.
- o Changes in the blink reflex.
- o Eyelids getting heavier.
- o Person becoming motionless.
- o Involuntary twitches of muscle.

In the next chapter, you will learn about powerful language patterns based on the Milton Model.

CHAPTER EIGHT:

The Milton Model's Powerful Influence

Milton Model Interpreted

The Milton Model is the prototype for suggestive hypnotic communication based on Milton Erickson's purposefully vague and ambiguous use of language that activates the client's subconscious and extracts its own interpretation of the message received. More specifically, the Milton Model is the medium of communication that can influence the client and their subconscious to act by deducing their own individual meaning of words that came up during a hypnosis or hypnotherapy session. The use of the Milton Model during hypnosis creates a state of focused attention in the client, with the client being preoccupied by their attempts at interpreting a meaning of non-specific language. This, in turn, creates a heightened state of suggestibility in the client, thanks to the Milton Model's use of "metaphors for artfully vague suggestions" (Excellence Assured, n.d.).

The Milton Model can be broken down further into three respective components that help the individual to understand its process. These three components are rapport, overloading conscious attention, and indirect communication ("Methods of Neuro-Linguistic Programming," 2019). These all work together to induce a trance by getting in touch with the subconscious of the individual. For example, the first component of **rapport** aids receptivity between the client and the hypnotist through certain NLP techniques, such as mirroring. This rapport is then what allows the hypnotist to lead the client in transforming their subjective state of mind, which then moves us toward the second component of the Milton Model: overloading the client's conscious attention.

Overloading the client's conscious attention is done by employing purposefully vague and ambiguous language that has the conscious mind trying to figure out the meaning of what was just said. This action then effectively diverts the attention of the person's conscious mind. It is this diversion that allows the subconscious mind to thrive, leading into the third component of the Milton Model, which is indirect communication.

Indirect communication, in this sense, not only accesses the subconscious mind, but also directs it into full awareness with the power of suggestion embedded in the language used during the hypnosis session. This is because the non-specific language allows the client to elicit their own meaning from it, which is why the Milton Model works like a charm. In the Milton Model, each respective component helps the other achieve success, specifically for changes and results that the client wants.

As mentioned, the Milton Model was influenced by Milton Erickson, who is considered the father of hypnotherapy. Erickson was a leading practitioner in his time, and involved himself in many professional endeavors related to his practice. Some of these professional endeavors include founding the American Society of Clinical Hypnosis, doing lectures and seminars, and running a private practice. Erickson kept himself engaged in his line of work as he was becoming renowned for his success.

In addition, the Milton Model mirrors Erickson's use of ambiguous language to make the client extract a meaning most appropriate for that individual and their current situation. This permitted Erickson to induce and make use of a person's trance and subsequently helping people conquer their problems and achieve practical results. Because of this success, Erickson was studied by Richard Bandler and John Grinder, who ultimately created The Milton Model in The Patterns of the Hypnotic Techniques by Milton Erickson.

Although the Milton Model is based on Erickson's work, Erickson himself had to learn from his colleagues in the field at the time as well. For example, Erickson learned to think highly of the client's subconscious mind and treat it with respect from having followed his colleagues' examples. Erickson also believed that there is a positive intention behind every action, and he based this belief on how people make the most beneficial choice they can time given the resources available to them. Another important thing to note is that Erickson held his client's reality in high esteem. Erickson clearly respected his clients, which may have influenced the general presupposition that there are no inflexible clients—only inflexible practitioners.

In short, the Milton Model was influenced by the man himself and is practiced in hypnotherapy. Since Erickson used vague and ambiguous language with his clients to achieve the desired results, so does his famous model. Erickson was the master at "providing the context with as little content as possible, so his clients could then paint the picture" (NLP World, n.d.). Similarly, the Milton Model ensures the most pertinent meaning is elicited from the language that frames the context.

Lastly, the Milton Model and its nonspecific but suggestive language is used so widely today in fields like psychology, law, business, and advertising that it is sometimes difficult to notice it in society, in part because we have been conditioned to accept it as commonplace. Therefore, the next time you go to the movies and watch the advertisements beforehand, take note of the vague and suggestive language used and how you react to them. Try your best to remain uninfluenced by them.

Milton Model's Powerful Language Patterns

Powerful language patterns in the Milton Model can structure, influence, and manipulate thoughts and behaviors just by their very existence. When we use and apply these powerful Milton Model language patterns to our daily lives or during a hypnosis session, our thinking begins to change. For instance, according to Elston, the receiver of that patterned message will begin to move into higher levels of thinking rather than simply detailing the content of their thinking (n.d.). In addition, inducing relaxation can occur when certain language patterns lead into it, and other Milton Model language patterns can help the client contemplate possibilities with a more extensive interpretation of the world. In other words, sometimes perspective can make all the difference.

Milton Model language patterns not only provide that perspective, but they are also a language of change that influences the client to take action. For example, the language pattern **cause-and-effect** suggests that one thing will lead to another via "If...then." This is helpful to know when the client needs to act or think about the effect something may cause if the hypnotist links the two ideas together in this pattern. Some other helpful Milton Model language patterns include (Elston, n.d.):

- **Mind Read**—Alleging to have knowledge of another's thoughts without detailing how you came to that knowledge.
  - o "I know you're thinking..."
- **Ambiguity**—Lack of specificity.
  - o Phonological: "you're" and "your"—same sound, different meaning.
- **Lost Performative**—Conveying value judgments without identifying the source of the judgment.
  - o "Walking is good."
- **Double Bind**—Invites choice, despite there really being no choice.
  - o "Do you want to talk now or later?"
- **Presupposition**—The linguistic equivalent of assumptions.
  - o "Will you be changing your perspective now or later today?"
- **Unspecified Verb**—Suggests action by alluding to how the action will take place.
  - o "She caused the issue."

- **Universal Quantifier**—Universal generalizations without referential index.
  - "Every; No One; All; Everyone"
- **Utilization**—Takes account of the entire listener's experience to support the speaker's intention.
  - Perhaps during a session, a colleague accidentally opens the door, the practitioner can say, "The opening door is an opportunity to invite new ideas into your life."
- **Embedded Commands**—A command forming a larger part of the sentence marked by body language changes that the listener's subconscious will pick up on.
  - "I will not imply that change is easy."
- **Comparative Deletion**—A comparison made without specific reference to what is being compared.
  - "You will like it more."

This list is by no means exhaustive, as there are many other powerful Milton Model language patterns to help guide the hypnotherapy session. It is important to note that although these powerful language patterns can be learned consciously, they are practiced and take place subconsciously, as language itself is a spontaneous and organic activity. In addition, using the Milton Model's language patterns would take at least a few years of practice for the user to become comfortable and fluent in applying them. Case in point, Erickson practiced for years to become adept at communicating to hundreds of clients and refining these powerful language patterns and techniques. In short, it is clearly important to practice as much as possible.

Just like learning a new language takes practice through written and oral communication and expression, so does learning to "speak hypnosis." It takes months of writing the language patterns down more than a few times a day, in addition to conversing fluently with the Milton Model language patterns. You will be most successful only when you can articulate these powerful language patterns with ease.

The language patterns in the Milton Model are applicable to just about any situation due to their use of non-specific language. Some of this non-specific language includes unspecified nouns and verbs, unspecified referential indices, and unspecified verbs and adverbs. Unspecified nouns and verbs compel the client to employ the imagination to fill in details such as the *who's* and *how's*. This is useful when the speaker becomes too detailed or specific, which could potentially decrease influence and break rapport. Secondly, the use of unspecified referential indices, like the word "this," compels us to guesstimate the specifics, in addition to making an internal decision about the sentence topic (Elston). Finally, the use of unspecified verbs and adverbs within the Milton Model of powerful language lets us fill in the context with our own experiences and knowledge. Unspecified language is leading and suggestive because it allows the client to deduce their own meaning and intentions from it, which then influences and guides the client even further.

It is clear that the powerful use of language within the Milton Model can shape and influence the direction, goals, and outcome of a hypnotherapy session, in addition to the client being influenced as a direct result. This is why it is critical to practice learning how to appropriately use the powerful language within the Milton Model. It is also important not to underestimate the potency of language, even if verbal language accounts for only a small part of communication. The verbal language used in therapy per the Milton Model makes the words count just as much as the non-verbal language that the client and the practitioner use during their interaction.

Chapter Summary

In this chapter, you learned all about the powerful language patterns the Milton Model uses to direct, guide, and influence therapy and the client. In addition, you learned about the Milton Model itself, plus its originator, Milton Erickson. To refresh your memory, here are the key points of this chapter:

- The Milton Model is the prototype for suggestive hypnotic communication, based on Milton Erickson's purposefully vague and ambiguous use of language that activated the client's subconscious and had it extract its own meaning and interpretation of the message received.
- The Milton Model's three components are rapport, overloading conscious attention, and indirect communication.
- The Milton Model was influenced by Milton Erickson, who is considered the father of hypnotherapy.
- The powerful language patterns within the Milton Model move our thinking toward higher levels, rather than simply detailing the content of our thinking.
- Some powerful language patterns of the Milton Model include:
  o Mind Read.
  o Ambiguity.
  o Lost Performative.
  o Double Blind.
  o Presupposition.
  o Unspecified Verbs.
  o Universal Quantifier.
  o Utilization.
  o Embedded Commands.
  o Comparative Deletion.
- One must practice learning to speak hypnosis through written and oral communication.
- Unspecified language can be leading and suggestive because it allows the client to deduce their own meaning and intentions from it, which then influences and guides them.

In the next chapter, you will learn about hypnotic conversations.

CHAPTER NINE:

Hypnotic Conversations

Power of Words

Words can be very powerful because they have the capacity to affect our subjective state of mind and everyday experiences by influencing our thoughts, behaviors, reactions, and actions. Words can even elicit emotions and evoke memories with their connotations and contextual interpretations. Words have the power to help us communicate and understand each other. In addition, words not only influence *what* we think, but also *how* we think, given they can structure one's mind through repeated conditioning. Without words, our world and experiences would be much different. In short, words are one of mankind's greatest achievements.

Words are so powerful that they can also trigger us consciously or subconsciously through the use of trigger words. **Trigger words**, loosely defined, are words that can incline an individual to take action. For example, certain verbs can be considered trigger words because they allude to an action, like the word "remember." When someone asks you to remember something, the action of being able to recall the past experience or event will trigger a memory. This can then evoke emotions that are associated with the memory. Trigger words are important to hypnosis because the individual's subjective state of mind can be influenced and manipulated with their use.

When someone uses words in a conversation to move you to react, respond, or act in a specific way, conversational hypnosis occurs. **Conversational hypnosis** is the use of trigger words in a conversation that can induce reactions, responses, and actions. The trigger words in a conversation are known to (NLP Training Dubai, n.d.):

- Activate our senses.
- Stimulate the imagination.
- Create associations and friendships.
- Help us visualize a specific picture in our minds, related to the words.
- Close deals.
- Bring relationships closer.
- Have the power to distract.
- Help us correlate ideas we otherwise may miss.

Conversational hypnosis allows us to communicate on a profound level, which helps us become more influential and persuasive by targeting the unconscious mind using body language, thoughts, and words. The use of **hot words** can bypass the critical factor and permeate the individual's subconscious because they are emotionally powerful enough to induce a strong response or reaction in the listener. For example, politicians, motivational speakers, and even your parents may use hot words to influence you to take action. Some hot words might include (Mcleod, 2009):

- Expletives.
- Value judgments about self.
- Sensory words.
- A named emotion.
- Precision words.
- Action words referring to the self.
- Extreme value judgments about others.

The power of words in my own experience has been one of transformation because, in learning about how to use and employ specific words in various situations, I can bring about positive changes to my life. Positive changes such as education, marriage, and even a career, as a result of the influential power of words has enriched my experience of life itself. It all comes down to how you use words that can change your life for the better. Especially in careers that make it their business to influence people, the power of words can determine whether a professional achieves success.

Hypnotic Power Words to Remember

Hypnotic power words are the kind we use every day. Whether you're talking to your partner, instant messaging your mom on Facebook, or writing a letter to your pen pal in another country, **hypnotic power words** are ordinary words woven into commonly used language. There is really nothing extraordinary about them. You don't have to have a degree or certification to use them, nor do you have to be a linguist to apply them. In fact, power words are simply run-of-the-mill, yet this is what makes them so special. This is because their frequent use in language and communication means they are more widely accepted and less challenged by people, meaning less resistance to their use. Therefore, what makes everyday words power words is not necessarily what you say, but how you say them.

As I mentioned in the previous chapter, power words or hypnotic power words are capable of inducing action. Some of those actions may include: activating our senses, stimulating our imagination, or correlating ideas. It is amazing how so much can happen based on everyday power words like the word "because;" for instance, *because I drank a lot of coffee, I am able to work more efficiently*. More specifically, the word "because" can help ideas correlate and flow more smoothly. This can be very useful in conversational hypnosis because it also aids the client in understanding cause-and-effect, in addition to creating useful associations.

Another hypnotic power word is the word "and." The word "and" can help ideas and thoughts build upon each other, painting a more detailed picture for the client. As you read this chapter, you'll gain more knowledge *and* skills. The word "and" is a useful conjunction that joins ideas and phrases, which can help the client to coordinate things into a relationship, establishing harmony and efficiency (Lexico, 2020). This is helpful to conversational hypnosis and everyday life because the word helps bring about agreement and concord from the individual.

In addition, the hypnotic power word "as" is another conjunction that is used to connect ideas. For example, *I will take breaks as I work.* This is helpful to conversational hypnosis because the word helps induce action, which can influence appropriate responses. For example, as you listen to the sound of rain falling on the ground, you can relax more deeply.

The word "imagine" is another powerful hypnotic word because it stimulates the individual's mind to visualize a scenario. For example, imagine yourself achieving success after you read this book. Even the rock and roll music group The Beatles wrote a masterpiece entitled, "Imagine." The word also allows the individual to experience the feelings or thoughts they want to have.

"Which means" is an effective power phrase to use in conversational hypnosis because it is used to explain or define something in more detail to the client. For example, *I will buy some more beads, which means I will make a bracelet with them.* The phrase "which means" determines the character of the noun preceding it and demonstrates the quantity, possession, or nearness to the speaker (Your Dictionary, n.d.). This is clearly helpful in conversational hypnosis because the individual will be able to understand more of what the hypnotist means by the latter being more specific in the second clause.

Conversational hypnosis has plenty more words to induce reaction, action, thoughts, and behaviors. Some other hypnotic power words to use include (Ledochowski, 2019):

- Just pretend.
- The more.
- Every time.
- What's it like when
- Supposed.
- Remember.
- What would it be like if.
- Find yourself.
- Realize.
- Sooner or later.

Hypnotic power words stimulate the unconscious mind and induce action of some kind, given their powerful influence through not only in what is said, but also in how it is said. In addition, hypnotic power words can frame the context for the individual, which can help guide and direct their thoughts, feelings, actions, and behaviors. This is useful to the hypnotist, who can then manipulate and control the client and the outcome of the hypnosis session.

Are You a Conversational Hypnotist?

Conversational hypnotists are experts at influencing everyone they meet. They know how to get you to do what they want because they are persuasive with their controlling and manipulative techniques. Their skills can work well on your unconscious mind, thoughts, feelings, and even behaviors. In short, conversational hypnotists know how to convince you to acquiesce to the will and agenda of others because they make use of their natural gifts as influencers. However, even the most skilled conversational hypnotist had to learn to master specific skills to win you over. For example, one of the crucial elements of persuasion is having the right mindset, which can make all the difference in determining if the situation is conducive to influence to begin with.

Another crucial aspect of successful conversational hypnotists is their ability to make use of influential power words, as they can give your presentation the power and energy it needs to make an impact. The right words can determine if and how your listener will respond to the message received. For example, words such as imagine, realize, and remember can initiate a sequence of events that trigger the subconscious into action. These words would do this by penetrating the region of the mind that is most likely to react to these words and their connotations.

The third crucial element of a conversational hypnotist is showing congruence between your body language, words, and thoughts. This is important because the listener will find you more believable and credible if your verbal and non-verbal body language matches each other. In other words, your words and actions have to be in sync; otherwise, the receiver of your message will be less likely to buy into whatever it is you're trying to convince them of. You can't be doing one thing while saying another.

A conversational hypnotist has many tools and techniques in their arsenal that can make or break the deal. Some more of those techniques include:

- Working on your attitude.
- Being consistent in what you say and do.
- Building rapport with the individual.
- Following the ABS Formula.
  - Absorb attention.
  - Bypass the critical factor.
  - Stimulate the unconscious mind.
- Captivating the individual with interesting stories.
- Making use of linguistic bridges (like and) and power words.
- Making use of hypnotic themes to set the mood.
- Inflaming things with the use of hot words (or emotive words).
- Learning how to recognize trance signals (Ledochowski, 2019):
  - Relaxed face.
  - Pupil dilation.
  - Breathing changes.
  - Heavy eyelids.
  - Lack of movement.

In order for these tools and techniques to work, it is important to establish a connection with the individual; otherwise, hypnosis may not be as effective, given the lack of association with the recipient. When this connection is established, then the conversational hypnotist can employ even more tools of the trade to influence and persuade the other person in the conversation. Such tools include (Radwan, 2017):

- **Pattern interrupt**—Interrupting regular patterns to program the mind of the person.
- **The Zeigarnik effect**—Telling someone an incomplete story to engage the conscious mind with hypnotic commands until the rest of the story is told.
- **Negative words**—The use of negative words to initiate the opposite action.
- **Ambiguity**—The use of ambiguous words to propel the subconscious mind into action.
- **Hypnotic keywords**—Programs the subconscious mind.

A conversational hypnotist definitely has many tools in their arsenal that they can use to influence and persuade; however, the most important tool is the words used to convey the message. Words can add depth, meaning, and context to the message, as well as define context and how it comes across to the listener. Since words have so much power and influence, it is important to use them with care because they can affect the individual on so many levels. In short, words do more than influence; they color the language with which we live our lives.

Chapter Summary

In this chapter, you have learned all about the power of words, their influence, and their use in conversational hypnosis. You have also learned that how something expressed through words is as important and valuable to what is expressed by those words. In addition, you have learned about hypnotic power words that can influence and direct a person's thoughts, feelings, actions, and behaviors. Remember that conversational hypnosis can control and manipulate your unconscious mind into action, suiting the will and agenda of the conversational hypnotist. The conversational hypnotist is a major factor for why we must use words with care. To refresh your memory, here are the key points of this chapter:

- Words have the power to affect our subjective state of mind and everyday experiences by influencing our thoughts, behaviors, reactions, and actions.
- Trigger words can stimulate the subconscious into action by inducing reactions and responses to what is said.
- Hypnotic power words can frame the context for the individual, which can then guide and direct their thoughts, feelings, actions, and behaviors.
- A conversational hypnotist's most important tool is the words used to convey their message because they add depth, meaning, and context to what is said.

In the next chapter, you will learn about NLP anchoring techniques.

CHAPTER TEN:

Persuasive NLP Anchoring Techniques

Anchoring Interpreted

Anchoring is a useful NLP technique that the NLP Practitioner can use during a session to induce a specific state of mind, emotion, or feeling in the client. With anchoring, they would be making use of a particular touch, word, or movement to allow the client to recall that desired feeling now and later. Another way to view NLP anchoring is that it is similar to bookmarking a specific website or a place in a book to return to it later. The only difference is that, instead of using the web browser or page to identify the desired destination, the NLP Practitioner would employ words and touch to signify the desired outcome, whether it be a feeling or state of mind. In short, NLP anchoring is similar to grounding oneself in a desired feeling or state of mind by associating it with something in the external environment, such as touch, object, or spoken word, so the person can experience it again.

Defining Anchoring

NLP anchoring is more distinctly defined by Mind Tools as "the process of linking an internal response with some external or internal trigger, so the response can be expeditiously summoned [again later]" (2019). It's almost as if a magician can conjure up a desired state of mind by snapping their fingers. In reality, anchoring is useful to the practice of NLP because it can put the individual in the right frame of mind to undergo even more therapeutic NLP techniques. Therefore, anchoring would help the person achieve their initial goals and the desired outcomes. NLP anchoring is conducive to setting the context during an NLP session and persuading the individual into taking a particular action. If I were to use the technique on myself, I could anchor the feeling of calm to the action of taking a deep breath, thus making myself more likely to recall that feeling after taking a deep breath when I am tense. As you can see, NLP anchoring can be very useful in many situations and contexts.

Background and History of NLP Anchoring

NLP anchoring has an interesting background and history. The development of NLP anchoring is likened to Ivan Pavlov's famous experiment on classical conditioning, in which he had dogs conditioned to salivate when they heard a bell chime. More specifically, if one constantly induces a behavioral response with a conditioned stimulus while another (neutral/unconditioned) stimulus is present, the response and the unconditioned stimulus will eventually correlate, creating a conditioned stimulus. After a while, the behavioral response will no longer require the original conditioned stimulus for the new one to cause that behavioral response. Back to the origin's main experiment, Pavlov's dogs were classically conditioned to expect food after hearing the ringing of a bell, and they eventually began to salivate whenever they heard the bell. Similarly, an individual undergoing NLP therapy can be classically conditioned to give a behavioral reaction once a stimulus materializes, such as a touch, word, or movement. After a while, the individual would associate that touch, word, or movement with the desired state of mind without the NLP Practitioner's assistance. NLP anchoring is a subtle form of classical conditioning, in which reactions or responses become automatic and reflexive after some time.

This conditioned automatic response via anchoring was first noted in Bandler and Grinder's book entitled, *Frogs into Princes* (1979). Their book is essentially a how-to describing the techniques for setting anchors and how they can affect positive change in our lives. The book is based off of Milton Erickson's masterful use of anchoring, especially with the auditory system, to change his clients' lives for the better. Erickson would use his vocal tone to induce trances in his clients and create human change innovatively. We could say that Erickson is the father of anchoring as well, although Pavlov may have influenced it to some degree.

Anchoring's Relevance in Daily Life and Marketing

The relevance of NLP anchoring today is that it constantly appears in our daily lives and across all aspects, like in marketing career fields. One way NLP anchoring is useful is in how it can condition us to respond more appropriately to a situation, event, or stimulus in our lives. For example, if you usually respond to hunger by grabbing the most convenient junk food you can find, try anchoring yourself to respond to hunger more appropriately by already having healthier snacks within reach. At first, it may be challenging to train or condition yourself to respond in healthier ways to stimulating situations or events, but with enough time and practice, anchoring can improve your life by giving you healthier ways to cope and manage any situation.

NLP anchoring is also useful within the field of marketing because products and services can be marketed through stimuli to recall a behavior and their product or service. For example, McDonald's golden arches might incline you to eat one of their cheeseburgers, due to the presence of the golden arches reminding you of their products and the behavior of eating. McDonald's has sold their products many times over with this logo. Another example would be the use of the Mayhem character from the Allstate commercials advertised on television. To explain, Mayhem's reckless behavior in Allstate commercials is the stimulus that makes you want to buy Allstate insurance, "so you can be better protected like me." The anchoring of reckless behavior to a character like Mayhem reminds us of the need for insurance, given

Mayhem's association to Allstate and human behavior. As a result, Allstate insurance has become even more successful in selling their products to consumers. In conclusion, anchoring can be used in a variety of contexts and for a variety of reasons.

Brain's Reaction to Anchoring

According to a study done at Rutgers University, the anchoring process in our brains can be described as:

> Engagement of cortical regions previously linked to emotional regulatory functions may be significant for enhancing or sustaining pleasant feelings during positive reminiscence, thus dampening the physiological stress response, therefore recalling happy memories elicits positive feelings and enhances one's well-being, suggesting a potential adaptive function in using this strategy for coping with stress.
>
> (James, 2017)

In other words, what happens in the brain during anchoring is a process in which the brain bypasses stress by using positive thoughts and memories to elicit positive feelings. This may also be due to the emotion and memory parts of the brain being in close proximity to each other via the hippocampus and amygdala. The neuroscience of anchoring is quite informative, and allows NLP Practitioners and everyday people to render stress effectively into more positive associations and outcomes.

NLP Anchoring Techniques Steps

Positive outcomes can be achieved with NLP anchoring techniques because they induce a positive state of mind in the individual. In addition, the classic NLP anchoring technique is not really that difficult, and anybody from the common person, to a salesperson, to a trained NLP Practitioner should be able to pull it off. Still, NLP anchoring must be done with the utmost care, consideration, and respect for the individual, similar to hypnosis in that regard. The person can be anchored by following some simple steps:

- **Step One**—Observe the state of mind built up in the individual.
- **Step Two**—Set the anchor by applying touch to a part of the individual's body, like the arm.
- **Step Three**—Practitioner holds the anchor for as long as the state is peaking, usually about 20-30 seconds.
- **Step Four**—Practitioner tests the anchor by applying the same touch to the same part of the body, in the same manner as before.
- **Step Six**—Observe the client to see if the same state originates when the touch is applied.

The practice of NLP anchoring can be very effective to elicit change in the individual because doing so allows that person to develop improved coping mechanisms and the internal resources. sp they can then deal with external events and situations. For example, a gentle pat on the back could elicit a positive state of mind to help me cope with challenging situations more efficiently. Now I've learned to associate a pat on the back with a positive state of mind and coping mechanisms via NLP anchoring.

When to Use NLP Anchoring

Anchoring is often used when the individual wants to attract, entice, tempt, or otherwise seduce a person into a specific state of mind or action that would suit the former's agenda. For example, if I wanted to entice you into buying one of my beaded bracelets, I would ask you about a happy memory. While you are recalling that memory, I would use a particular gesture or touch to anchor or ground you to that happy memory and the emotions associated with it. That way, you would be more likely to purchase my beaded jewelry because happy feelings are associated with the gesture and my person. As a result, you will associate the happy feelings with being around me now, due to the transfer of it from your person to mine. It is a trick that can swindle the individual of those happy feelings associated with the memory, unless they associate it with the individual doing the anchoring.

NLP Anchoring Process

The anchoring process might seem pretty simple, but there is a science to doing it correctly. For example, the individual must completely access the state of mind with clarity; otherwise, anchoring becomes less effective. In addition, the NLP Practitioner has to observe their client keenly to notice when that state of mind peaks at its strongest, or else the anchor won't work. A failed anchor can occur if there is less emotion or lack of state of mind to associate it to. The third step in the anchoring process requires the NLP Practitioner to break the state by disengaging the touch or word. This has to be done carefully because the individual coming out of that specific state might be a bit disoriented. Last but not least is the fourth step to the anchoring process, which is to fire the anchor to test it. This means the NLP Practitioner has to use the same touch or word to initiate the state of mind again to see if it works. The NLP Practitioner has to be spot-on when testing the anchor; otherwise, it won't seem as natural to the individual. Remember the four steps to the anchoring process are:

- Coax the individual into accessing the state of mind.
- Provide an anchor as the state peaks.
- Break that state by disengaging.
- Test the anchor again to see if it works.

The anchoring process is a delicate operation because nuances in body language, tone of voice, and even behavior can throw off the attempt to anchor. This is why the anchoring process requires congruence in body language from the NLP Practitioner. The associations and connections made from anchoring depend on it because then the NLP Practitioner can appear more credible to the individual.

The Different Forms of Anchoring in NLP

The different forms of anchoring are unique and specific to each individual situation. For example, **stacking an anchor** is when the NLP Practitioner has the individual access many different experiences that elicit the same state of mind, so the NLP Coach can anchor the experiences in the same place (Carroll, 2013). This strategy is useful because it helps the client learn to deal with those experiences effectively by tying them all together. This technique could work well for dealing with negative experiences, too.

Another form of anchoring is collapsing anchors. **Collapsing anchors** involves the NLP Coach helping the client acquire a resourceful state when there previously wasn't one, due to a context in which the client lacked choices. This is achieved by anchoring the unresourceful state of mind to a particular place, whereas the resourceful state becomes anchored to a different place. It is helpful to have two different anchors representing various states on different sides of the body because it will be easier to collapse the unresourceful state into the resourceful state. This is done by firing the two independent anchors at the same time, then releasing the unresourceful anchor before the resourceful one. The NLP Coach can then test the strength of the resourceful anchor by firing it. If the response is the same as before when the resourceful anchor was initiated, then the NLP Coach has succeeded in creating a resourceful state for the client.

The third form of anchoring is chaining anchors. **Chaining anchors** happens when the unresourceful state is too big in size to collapse, making it necessary to create an intermediate state akin to a bridge between the beginning state and the end state. If the anchors are chained properly, one will lead to the next when fired, allowing the client to build a bridge or link between various states. This is helpful to the client because it can lead the individual to the desired state, especially when the states are very different from one another.

Another form of anchoring is sliding anchors. **Sliding anchors** are necessary when the NLP Practitioner or Coach must calibrate the intensity of the individual's state without stacking them; the method which was described previously. For example, a sliding anchor will depend on the NLP Practitioner's touch point, matching the intensity of the individual's state of mind. This is useful to the individual because overwhelming or strong feelings can be controlled or manipulated to the desired strength the client wants.

Last but not least are spatial anchors. **Spatial anchors** can be manipulated or controlled without touch; instead, it is done spatially by the NLP Practitioner or Coach. For example, to imitate or represent stacking anchors, the NLP Practitioner would access the resource state repeatedly by physically stepping into the appointed anchoring space. Sometimes, it can help the client to see a physical representation to understand the process of anchoring itself.

NLP Anchoring Techniques in Sales

Anchoring techniques in sales evoke specific responses, which then lead to the closing of the sale by the means of an anchor or trigger, producing a response in the individual. That anchor or trigger could be a specific word or a touch that persuades the individual to purchase your product or service. For example, if I use shaking your hands to introduce myself when selling Girl Scout cookies, I could trigger you into buying them with a persuasive smile and conversation. In addition, some more specific anchoring techniques in sales include the use of spatial anchors, anchoring state elicitation, anchor chain, and price anchoring.

The first anchoring sales technique uses physical actions and gestures to evoke emotional responses and overcome objections. For example, I could step into your personal space and smile as I try to sell you my product. In fact, using **spatial anchors** to overcome objections to the sale reminds me of salespeople at the mall trying to invade your personal space and sell you a product. This is because, as you try to walk by them, they would sometimes invade your personal space first to give you a sample of what they are trying to sell; they may try to spray some perfume or cologne on you to get you to overcome any objections you may have of buying it, for example.

The second anchoring sales technique, **state elicitation**, connects a physical object to an emotional state. For example, I could connect the remote control to my interest in watching my favorite shows on television. By connecting the remote control with excitement in watching Star Trek, I can evoke this emotional state by simply presenting the remote control. Another example is the use of my coffee cup at work because I can connect it to feeling productive (given the caffeine). By simply seeing the coffee cup, a feeling or productivity resonates in me and I work more efficiently.

The third anchoring sales technique is using an **anchor chain**, which involves moving an audience from one state to another by use of spatial anchors. For example, I could link emotional states to spatial anchors and shift between them when I want my audience to shift their state of mind. Stepping to the right could indicate understanding, whereas stepping to the left could indicate agreement.

The fourth anchoring sales technique is **price anchoring**, which is when the price of one product is compared to another, more expensive one to convince you to buy the more expensive product. For example, "Similar laptops sell for $300, $400, or even $500! But you can get this laptop for only $199.99!" Consumers will think they are getting a deal because the price is anchored higher than what it is selling for. In conclusion, anchoring sales techniques can be very effective to trick you into purchasing a product or service being sold.

The Art of Anchoring and Mind Control

Anchoring and mind control requires the use of language patterns to act as triggers or anchors that influence and control our responses, which then also influences us to do things without our knowledge, consent, or awareness. This is partly because these linguistic anchors have been conditioned into our minds from birth, making it challenging for the average individual to discern them and the reactions they cause. For example, the word "no" can act as an anchor or trigger for negative experiences, associations, and states of mind. Be that as it may, mind control through the anchoring of language patterns can also influence our lives beneficially.

Anchoring Used to Attract Women

The skill of attracting a woman through anchoring can be a nuanced endeavor, depending on certain variables such as personality, mindset, context, compatibility, and whether she likes you to begin with. In fact, using anchoring to attract a woman will not work if none of these variables are in place. If there is a mutual attraction, then anchoring will have a higher chance of being successful in this field. The two kinds of anchoring most widely used to attract and keep a woman are emotional anchoring and expectation anchoring. We will talk about these more in detail in the next sections.

Emotional anchoring is when a woman is conditioned to feel specific emotions relating to you, an object, or a situation. In other words, emotional anchoring is when the woman connects the emotions she feels to you whenever she is in your presence (Amante, 2020). For example, if a woman meets you at a festival, then she will probably start associating with you the feelings of excitement she had when she met you in that specific context. On the other hand, if a woman met you at the library during the day, she might associate calmer feelings with you. Knowing this can be useful for setting up a date with her because she may be more likely to want to see you again if the anchor fits.

As mentioned, the second kind of anchoring used to attract a woman is expectation anchoring. **Expectation anchoring** is when you anchor to yourself an expectation, so the woman can expect or associate it with you. For example, if you tell her, "We should get coffee sometime," she will probably expect a date with you in the near future. In addition, it is okay to raise or lower expectations depending on the situation. Expectation anchoring can determine the course of a relationship because "whatever expectation you anchor to her is what she is going to expect from you" (Amante, 2020). In conclusion, you can use the art of anchoring to attract a woman, given the right conditions.

Anchoring Used in Sales

To use anchoring in sales, the salesperson must undertake a few actions to seal the deal. Those actions can make the chosen anchors work for the salesperson by (Woodley, n.d.):

- Convincing the individual to experience the appropriate emotion.
- Assisting the individual into that emotion, perhaps by amplifying it.
- Attaching an anchor—like a location, tone of voice, or movement—to the emotion.
- Directing the conversation away from the main topic into other topics.
- Employing the anchor at the right time to recreate the emotional experience you desire your client to have.

Anchoring used in sales can be effective because it ties emotions to the specific anchor, which then persuades and leads the individual into closing the deal. This is obviously good for business. It is the practice of anchoring in sales that determines whether a business thrives or simply survives.

Chapter Summary

In this chapter, you have learned all about anchoring. You have learned about its definition, history, and relevance in both daily life and marketing. In addition, you have learned how and when to use NLP anchoring. It is also important to note the anchoring process itself, along with its various formats. Lastly, you have learned about the art of anchoring and mind control via its applications in attracting women and increasing sales. To refresh your memory, here are the key points of this chapter:

- NLP anchoring is similar to grounding yourself in a desired feeling or state of mind by associating it with something in the external environment, like a touch, object, or spoken word, so you can experience it again.
- NLP anchoring is similar to classical conditioning.
- NLP anchoring is useful to marketing because products can be marketed by the use of a stimulus to recall a behavior associated with that stimulus and the product or service.
- NLP anchoring can be effective in eliciting change in an individual because it allows the person to develop improved coping mechanisms and the internal resources to deal with external events and situations.
- Anchoring is often used when the individual wants to attract, entice, tempt, or seduce someone into a specific state of mind or action that suits their agenda.
- The four steps to the anchoring process are:
  o Coax the individual into accessing that state of mind.
  o Provide an anchor as the state peaks.
  o Disengage to break that state.
  o Test the anchor again to see if it works.
- Different forms of anchoring include:
  o Stacking anchors.
  o Collapsing anchors.
  o Chaining anchors.
  o Sliding anchors.
  o Spatial anchors.
- Using emotional and expectation anchoring can help with attracting women.

- Anchoring used in sales is effective because it ties emotions to the specific anchor, which then persuades and leads the individual into closing the deal.
- Anchoring techniques in sales evoke specific responses, which then lead to closing the sale by the means of an anchor or trigger, producing a response in the individual.
- The four anchoring sales techniques are:
  o Spatial anchors.
  o Anchoring state elicitation.
  o Chain anchors.
  o Price anchoring.
- Anchoring in sales involves:
  o Convincing the individual into experiencing the appropriate emotion.
  o Assisting the individual into that emotion, perhaps by amplifying it.
  o Attaching an anchor, like a location, tone of voice, or movement, to the emotion.
  o Directing the conversation away from the main topic into other topics.
  o Employing the anchor at the right time to recreate the emotional experience you desire your client to have.

In the bonus chapter, you will learn about some more NLP techniques that anyone can use.

CHAPTER ELEVEN:

Bonus Chapter — More Suggestive NLP Techniques

NLP for Business

The inception of NLP in many businesses has created a higher degree of success because it teaches business people to become better communicators, thus bringing in more clients, sales, and profit. The NLP practice in business allows the business itself to thrive because productivity increases as a result when people can communicate more effectively within. In addition, being able to communicate more effectively will allow the brand message to be conveyed with more emphasis to potential prospects.

According to Lenka Lutonska, NLP is like an "SOP for the mind, allowing for progressive communication, that provides applications in leadership, marketing, and sales" (Barratt, 2019). This progressive communication can then lead to successful companies experiencing more returns than most. In other words, it pays to learn how to become a more effective communicator, which is necessary in today's business market, due to increased competition, informativeness of the Internet, online communication, and advertising.

Top Three Easy-to-Incorporate NLP Tips

Effective communication begins with learning some simple communication solutions that can transform your business into a more successful one in time. These solutions and skills involve learning to articulate in the same manner as your client, viewing things from a different point of view, and reviewing your beliefs to examine their relevance to the situation. The first skill of learning to adopt the same language as your client is very useful because the client will not only feel more understood but also more willing to acquiesce to your business requests. Once the client's preferred representational system is known, speak and articulate in the same manner. For example, if your client expresses themselves in more a visual manner, perhaps try using diagrams to get your point across.

The second skill of viewing things from a different point of view is helpful to business because doing so allows the professional to detach from the situation, due to there being more objectivity from seeing the situation for what it is. For example, once the professional giving a presentation can view things from the audience's point of view, the business person becomes more likely to place themselves in an objective observer's mindset. This can then set in motion improved product launches, sales conversations, and even presentations.

The third skill of reviewing your beliefs and examining their relevance is also important because doing so allows the business person to overcome their limited assumptions by first identifying the belief to deconstruct it. Otherwise, limiting beliefs and assumptions can affect our wellbeing negatively and, consequently, our performance in business and other areas of life. This calls for even more NLP techniques to help change those beliefs into something more constructive and beneficial. It is clear that effective communication with these three solutions will help your business in becoming more successful.

Language Pattern to Bypass Objection

The use of specific language patterns to bypass resistance, especially in sales, is incredibly useful to garner success in any business. The trick is to understand the motivation behind the objection, choice, or action; more specifically, if you can understand the individual's beliefs that make them think, talk, or act in a specific way, then you can understand what they are saying in a conversation, and even switch it around on them if necessary. For example, if April the salesperson was trying to sell her product, and she heard an objection from the prospective buyer, she would simply try to discover the motivation behind the objection by asking herself about the prospective buyer's beliefs that make them think, talk, or act that way. It is clearly helpful to learn the underlying motive or truth for the comment, behavior, or belief.

Beyond that, recognizing this aspect can then allow you to present the information differently by rephrasing it to suit the motivation behind the objection. For example, instead of sounding confrontational by jumping straight into the issue, try rewording the question or sentence non-threateningly and rechecking your understanding. You can ask yourself, "Can I check if I understand this properly?" then go into the issue, perhaps by making a comparison suggesting that changing the situation, instead of letting it stay the same, would be less difficult, given the consequences. This also helps the business person check their solution against what they think the prospective client is or isn't doing.

NLP in Building Relationships

The use of NLP in building and maintaining relationships is valuable and beneficial to the people involved because it can help them communicate and understand each other better. When the people in a relationship communicate and understand each other better, then the relationship itself will improve because the quality of the connection and interactions will increase many times over. This is where NLP comes into the picture because it will give you insight and knowledge into how

119

the human mind and the resulting behavior works to affect each other. In other words, NLP techniques can facilitate how we think, feel, react, respond, and act in relationships, which can then help improve communication within them while also aiding them to run more smoothly.

Some helpful ways in which NLP techniques can build and maintain relationships include choosing the right partner, listening to your partner, building rapport, and releasing your passion or emotions. For example, choosing the right partner for yourself becomes easier when you have an awareness of your own internal map and preferred representational system because self-knowledge can help you decide if another person's internal map and preferred representational system are compatible with yours.

There is great value in listening to your partner and hearing what they have to say. If you listen openly to your partner without judgment, they can feel more understood and validated, simply because you gave them your attention and time. Taking the time to listen can help the relationship in a variety of ways because you will be better able to discern the intended meaning of the message, which would then facilitate the relationship.

The NLP technique of building rapport with the client is also useful in building and maintaining other relationships as well. This is because it can garner trust, support, and confidence in the people within the relationship, whether that relationship be romantic, platonic, or familial. In addition, building rapport with your partner can show you have interest in them, which can then lead into a deeper relationship. Also important to note is that, since building rapport elicits trust between the people in a relationship, personal walls or boundaries can disappear, allowing people to be themselves in the relationship.

Finally, the use of NLP techniques in personal relationships can help build and maintain them by teaching the people in the relationship to release their emotions and passions in safe and healthy ways. For example, the NLP technique of releasing a kinesthetic anchor can keep the relationship exciting and remind the people in the relationship how much they are cared for, valued, and loved.

Attracting a Man with NLP

Attracting a man through the use of NLP is similar to training him to respond to you appropriately. This period of training could involve improving communication and seduction skills by using NLP techniques, such as mirroring, to increase rapport with him. Another NLP technique that can attract and seduce a man is speaking to him purposely slow and rhythmically, which would pull him in to listen to what you have to say. This strategy works because using your tone of voice can set the mood for the interaction to occur. Some more subtle NLP techniques to attract a man also include matching/mirroring your feelings to his when he expresses them in a conversation or otherwise. For example, if he says he is feeling happy because it is Friday, you can smile and say something like, "The end of the work week makes me happy, too." Especially valuable to attracting a man is anchoring because with the technique, you can get him to associate whatever positive feelings he has to being around you, be it a touch, look, or word. In conclusion, attracting a man with the use of NLP techniques can be very effective in winning his heart.

NLP VAKOG Brain Code in a Relationship

NLP can help relationships flourish and thrive because its practice is effective in bringing people closer to understanding each other on a deeper level, which then promotes the feelings, reactions, responses, and actions within it. NLP can also help facilitate relationships by understanding your own and your partner's preferred representational system or sensory modality whenever they communicate with you. For example, if your partner uses a visual system primarily, then the person will need to *see* your expression of love. If you are a kinesthetic-minded individual, you will need to *feel* the love to believe it. These various

121

sensory modalities can be described in NLP as "**The Brain Code, V-A-K-O-G** (**V**isual-**A**uditory-**K**inesthetic-**O**lfactory-**G**ustatory)" (Moghazy, 2018). This code is relevant to know because knowing these sensory modalities can help you match up with an individual who has the same preferred sensory modality, or at least one that is complementary. Similarly the **NLP VAK model** represents the three interpersonal communication modalities in which we communicate the language of love (Bundrant, n.d.). Knowing which interpersonal communication modality you and your partner each prefer can help the relationship blossom.

Unleashing the Power of the Subconscious in NLP Techniques

Using the power of the subconscious mind in tangent with NLP techniques is critical because our subconscious influences, manipulates, and controls every aspect of our lives, from emotions, to thoughts, to behaviors. In addition, the subconscious acts as a locus of control that guides your conscious mind, the latter of which then communicates back to the subconscious. Although communication is bidirectional, we need the conscious part of the mind to influence the subconscious part because it will help you influence your life to operate in the direction of your goals.

One way to influence the subconscious mind into enhancing life is to purge negative-self talk and fear; you can accomplish this task by using the countering or delete button techniques. According to Mayer, **countering** a negative thought is possible by replacing it with a positive thought, which will help your mind to make positive associations instead of negative ones (2018). In addition, the **delete button technique** is when you visualize pushing a delete button in your mind to destroy the negative thought. Both of these techniques are effective in influencing the subconscious.

Another way to spur the subconscious mind into more activity is to learn how to harness and foster your desire so you can use it to achieve your dreams. This is accomplished by using the bridge-burning, small wins or progress bar, and motivational techniques. The **bridge-burning technique** is immensely helpful because, by figuratively burning the bridges in your mind, you dismantle the safe, predictable harbors at either end of the bridge, thereby leading yourself into one direction only: forward. The **small wins** or **progress bar technique** allows the individual to keep track of smaller wins in light of bigger goals, which can make your process appear motivational for you, especially if you can see the bigger picture. Last but not least is the **motivational technique**, which has you discover what motivates you and can give you the energy to work toward your goal (Mayer, 2018).

Unlocking the subconscious mind is easier when you can visualize or picture the outcome of the goal ahead of time. This is because doing so will put you in the mindset of already having achieved it, which can then be effective for cultivating the desire of doing it in real time. Imagine yourself succeeding, then ask yourself the following questions:

- What am I doing?
- What am I wearing?
- What am I saying and feeling?
- How do I act?

Imagining this reality will guide you toward the desired outcome.

Some additional techniques for unlocking the subconscious to fulfill your dreams are **autosuggestions**, which are a way of "introducing thoughts to the subconscious mind" (Mayer, 2018). For example, take the mantra technique and the reading out loud technique. The powerful **mantra technique** of vocalizing or thinking repeatedly about a positive mantra like, "I can do more than I think," is helpful in achieving your goals because the more you repeat it, the more you will believe it. Restating your goals is the power of mantras, which is great for convincing your mind. Similarly, by stating and vocalizing your goals several times a day via reading them out loud, it reinforces your desire to accomplish the goal and desired outcome. The more techniques there are for unleashing the power of the subconscious, the better!

The Power of Autosuggestion in NLP

Autosuggestion is a powerful NLP technique that unlocks the subconscious by having the person present the thoughts they need to accomplish their goals to themselves. We do this all the time; for instance, I may say to myself that I need to focus more on the task at hand and, in turn, my focus will increase. Another autosuggestion could be to smile more by instructing yourself to smile at everyone you meet. Autosuggestions are effective in eliciting the desired state of mind, so you can eventually accomplish the objective.

Some more autosuggestion techniques are ones I have already mentioned, including the use of repetition and visualization to tap into your self-administered subconscious mind programming. Another technique is the use of affirmations. Affirmations or positive self-talk uses the present tense stated in the first person to allow the individual to reprogram their mind to think more positively, which can then guide their behavior in more positive directions. This form of self-suggestion is obviously beneficial because the individual's state of mind will determine their behavior and thoughts, thus influencing their life.

Autosuggestion can be a powerful form of self-hypnosis if done correctly. To engage in this technique, it is important at first to identify what you want to change, which will motivate you and give you a goal to work toward. The second step for engaging in autosuggestion is to relax yourself because it will let you become more open to suggestion, especially autosuggestion. The third step is to believe in yourself, as doing so will guide you toward positive thoughts and outcomes, as compared to the opposite. The fourth step is to simply feel your emotions, since their strength will influence your subconscious beneficially. The fifth step for engaging in autosuggestion is to think positively because doing so will get your subconscious to respond by the means of self-administering positive commands. In other words, you think; therefore, you are. The sixth and final step is to constantly practice the autosuggestion anytime you can, until you are one with it. In conclusion, autosuggestion is a great technique for reprogramming your mind through self-hypnosis and creating positive change.

Some other forms of autosuggestion include (Wise Goals, n.d.):

- Creating your own catchy statements to encourage yourself toward change.
- Changing one word in the autosuggestion to make it kinder.
- Playing the detective can help differentiate between opinion and fact.
- Using memorabilia to relish the past, creating positive emotions and affecting change.

Autosuggestion can help you implement a goal-setting mindset because it can reframe your thinking by creating a different state of mind or context from which to work from. This will ultimately help the individual to support themselves and the effort to create positive change. Another important tip to remember is that positive self-talk will improve your performance as you work toward achieving the desired goal and outcomes. In other words, you will feel motivated to do your best in working toward your goals. The third tip to remember regarding autosuggestion is that visualizing the goal will help you picture it, which attracts the reality of it into your life (Sukhia, n.d.). If you can see it, you can believe it! Also, important to note is that powerful people possess the power to effect positive change.

Re-aligning a Sense of True Power in NLP for Real Success

Re-aligning a sense of true power in NLP for real success involves priming the mind to consider the best that life has to offer by using pure motives such as love, compassion, and empathy. On the other hand, the use of selfish, self-promoting motives, like material gain, as the rationalization for practicing NLP can ultimately disrupt the natural laws of the universe by creating an imbalance of resources and power. This will only serve to affect the same intentions and motives you put out; therefore, to create true change, we must embody and personify positive values, such as integrity, to make a real difference.

Chapter Summary

In this chapter, you have learned all about other NLP techniques that can be applied and practiced in a variety of situations and contexts. For example, the practice and application of NLP techniques can be useful in business, personal relationships, and even yourself. To refresh your memory, here are the key points of this chapter:

- NLP in businesses can create success because it teaches people how to be better communicators, thus bringing in more clients, sales, and profit.
- The top three communication hacks in business via NLP are:
  o Speaking the same language as your client.
  o Viewing things from a different perspective.
  o Examining your beliefs.
- Some language patterns to bypass objections when marketing or selling a product are:
  o Learn and understand the underlying motive or truth for the comment, behavior, or belief.
  o Present the information differently by rephrasing it to suit the motivation behind the objection, choice, or action.
  o Check your understanding by re-wording the sentence, phrase, or issue non-threateningly.
  o Make a comparison suggesting that changing the situation, instead of staying the same, would be less difficult, given the consequences of staying the same per the objection.

- NLP techniques facilitate how we think, feel, and act in relationships, which can help them run more smoothly and improve communications.
- Some helpful ways that NLP techniques help build and maintain relationships include:
  o Choosing the right partner.
  o Listening to your partner.
  o Building rapport.
  o Releasing your passion or emotions.
- Attracting a man through NLP is similar to training him to respond to you appropriately via techniques like mirroring.
- NLP helps facilitate relationships by understanding yours and your partner's preferred representational system or sensory modality when they communicate with you.
- Understanding VAKOG (Visual-Auditory-Kinesthetic-Olfactory-Gustatory) can help your love life by helping you understand which sensory modality you and your partner prefer.
- Unleashing the power of the subconscious mind with NLP techniques is critical because the subconscious influences, manipulates, and controls every aspect of your life, from emotions, to thoughts, to behaviors.
- NLP techniques to unlock the power of the subconscious mind include:
  o Purging negative-self talk and fear by using the countering or delete button techniques.
  o Harnessing and fostering your desire to achieve your dreams is done by using the bridge-burning, small wins or progress bar, and the motivational techniques.
  o Visualizing or picturing the outcome of your goal ahead of time can help it become a reality.
  o Autosuggestions introduce thoughts to the subconscious mind by:
    ▪ Repetition.
    ▪ Visualization.
    ▪ Creating your own catchy statements.

- Changing a word in the autosuggestion to make it kinder.
- Playing the detective to differentiate between opinion and fact.
- Using memorabilia to create positive emotions that can affect positive change.

- Autosuggestion helps to implement a goal-setting mindset because it can reframe your thinking by creating a different state of mind or context from which to work toward your goals and dreams.
- Re-aligning a sense of true power in NLP for real success involves priming the mind to consider the best that life has to offer; it does this by using pure motives such as love, compassion, and empathy.

FINAL WORDS

Although the use of NLP is controversial, it is also beneficial to anyone who decides to apply it to their situation. NLP, or neuro-linguistic programming, can be helpful for relationships, business, and the people because its practice and application can create successful outcomes, no matter the context. There are environmental influences that can affect the practice of NLP, such as rationalizing its use for personal gain and power. Even so, NLP can help us to effectively adapt to the many environments or contexts we find ourselves in by reprogramming the mind to develop, progress, and evolve into a more functional instrument, thanks to the power of suggestion, influence, and persuasion. In short, NLP is useful because it can change how we think, perceive, react, and respond to life's challenges.

The mindful use and practice of NLP can put power back into your own hands by helping you control your mind and achieve favorable outcomes. In addition, NLP can help you to align your programming and beliefs with your own success, and not against it. For example, the practice of self-hypnosis enables people to introduce constructive thoughts into the unconscious by using specific NLP techniques, such as autosuggestion and anchoring. Other NLP techniques, like hypnotic power words, can stimulate the subconscious into action by inducing reactions that can directly influence our thoughts, behaviors, and feelings. Also important to note is NLP framing because of its ability to transform a person's mind by restructuring the limbic system links between the amygdala and the hippocampus, thus also changing the person's reality.

The evolving science of NLP is proving to be useful in fields such as psychology because it produces tangible results with how it can influence, manipulate, and control people. For instance, according to Zaharia, Reiner, and Schutz, in a study that "measured the level of anxiety in fifty participants with claustrophobia, anxiety scores significantly reduced after NLP sessions during the MRI examination" (2015). It is clear that NLP produces efficient and valuable results in a variety of contexts and situations.

The real power of NLP is evident in the topics and knowledge presented throughout this book. We have looked at how it can be applied in real world applications and examples. By shedding light upon the subject and practice of NLP, you are now more informed and ready to take action yourself to improve your life, and the lives of those you care for. It is up to you to decide how you use and apply this information, but I would err on the side of caution because mind programming is serious business that can also potentially hurt, beyond its healing properties. For example, the many cults that take advantage of the individual by manipulation and subterfuge.

Studying and practicing the NLP techniques present in this book will allow you to take control of your own life while you learn how to harness the power of your subconscious. You do this to influence and guide your thoughts, feelings, and behaviors more constructively and successfully. By taking control of your own mind, others with more malicious intentions will be less likely to manipulate and control you as well.

The potential of NLP to improve lives is unlimited and boundless. This is in part because NLP is versatile and adaptive to a variety of situations, contexts, and people. In addition, NLP itself is more open-ended and less structured, allowing for more self-directed opportunities like teaching yourself to think more positively. It is these self-directed opportunities that allow you to take control of your destiny by choosing to manipulate your mind and the outward manifestations of it. Once you make that choice, NLP is no longer a manipulative tool, but a helpful medium to change the course of your life.

Your life will change once you are more open to its opportunities via NLP because you now understand that what you do affects your mind, and your mind affects what you do. This relationship's bidirectional and interrelated nature allows you to focus mindfully on the present and learn to make better decisions later on.

NLP is a powerful tool of change that can create positive realities by inducing newer, more efficient ways for you to adapt and acclimate to your surroundings and events. By changing the context via reprogramming your mind, you can change the picture. A different perspective allows our thoughts, behaviors, and feelings to shift toward a more positive direction, serving to benefit our goals and fulfill our dreams. It is this shift that helps NLP guide its reception by reprogramming the mind to respond more appropriately to the picture itself.

If you want to be an agent of change, then NLP is the catalyst to make it happen. All it takes is a little bit of integrity, compassion, and empathy for you and everyone around you. Yet, to deal with change effectively, you must be open to it to begin with, which is where NLP can offer you tools to make that happen. Being open to suggestion, change, and influence can greatly improve your life trajectory; a trajectory in which you are no longer a victim of circumstance, but an empowered agent of change.

RESOURCES

Amante, C. (n.d.). How to use anchoring to mesmerize women. *Girls Chase*. Retrieved February 19, 2020 from https://www.girlschase.com/content/how-use-anchoring-mesmerize-women

Anchoring. (2019). *NLP World.* Retrieved February 19, 2020 from https://www.nlpworld.co.uk/nlp-glossary/a/anchoring/

Anchoring: NLP technique (n.d.). *NLP Secrets.* Retrieved February 19, 2020 from https://www.nlp-secrets.com/nlp-technique-anchoring.php

Andriessen, E. (2010). The philosophy and ethics of neuro linguistic programming. *The Princeton Tri-State Center for NLP.* Retrieved February 7, 2020 from https://nlpprinceton.com/the-philosophy-and-ethics-of-neuro-linguistic-programming-nlp/

Babich, N. (2016). How to detect lies: Micro expressions. *Medium.* Retrieved February 12, 2020 from https://medium.com/@101/how-to-detect-lies-microexpressions-b17ae1b1181e

Bandler, R. (2009). Messing with your head: Does the man behind neuro-linguistic programming want to change your life - Or control your mind? *Independent.* Retrieved February 7, 2020 from https://www.independent.co.uk/life-style/health-and-families/healthy-living/messing-with-your-head-does-the-man-behind-neuro-linguistic-programming-want-to-change-your-life-1774383.html

Barratt, B. (2019). 3 basic NLP techniques to bring more success to your business. *Forbes.* Retrieved February 20, 2020 from https://www.forbes.com/sites/biancabarratt/2019/07/11/3-basic-nlp-techniques-to-bring-more-success-to-your-business/#17fd0b063078

Bass, M. (n.d.). 5 powerful auto suggestion techniques to take control of your life. *Mind to Succeed.* Retrieved February 20, 2020 from https://www.mindtosucceed.com/auto-suggestion-techniques.html

Basu, R. (2016). Frame control, stealing your mind back. *The NLP company.* Retrieved February 14, 2020 from http://www.thenlpcompany.com/case-study/stealing-your-mind-back/

Beale, M. (2020). NLP techniques: 85+ essential neuro linguistic programming techniques. *NLP Techniques: Neuro-Linguistic Programming Techniques.* Retrieved February 8, 2020 from https://www.nlp-techniques.org

Body language secret: How to spot a bored person. (n.d.). *Mentalizer Education.* Retrieved February 11, 2020 from https://mentalizer.com/body-language-secret-how-to-spot-a-bored-person.html

Bored body language. (n.d.) *Changing Minds*. Retrieved February 11, 2020 from
   http://changingminds.org/techniques/body/bored_body.htm

Bradberry, T. (2017). 8 ways to read someone's body language. *Inc.* Retrieved
   February 9, 2020 from https://www.inc.com/travis-bradberry/8-great-tricks-for-
   reading-peoples-body-language.html

Bundrant, H. (n.d.). What is neuro-linguistic programming - NLP - And why learn it?
   iNLP. Retrieved February 6, 2020 from https://inlpcenter.org/what-is-neuro-
   linguistic-programming-nlp

Bundrant, M. (n.d.). Controlling people: Nine subtle ways you give others too much
   power. *iNLP*. Retrieved February 9, 2020 from https://inlpcenter.org/everyone-
   tries-to-control-me/

Bundrant, M. (n.d.). Love languages of NLP - Using VAK to increase awareness.
   iNLP. Retrieved February 20, 2020 from https://inlpcenter.org/love-languages/

Bundrant, M. (n.d.). NLP eye movements: Can you tell when someone is lying? *iNLP*.
   Retrieved February 9, 2020 from https://inlpcenter.org/chunk/coaching-exercise-
   eye-accessing-cues-business-making-decisions-solving-problems-2/

Campbell, S. (2017). How to use autosuggestion effectively, the definitive guide.
   Unstoppable Rise. Retrieved February 20, 2020 from
   https://www.unstoppablerise.com/autosuggestion-guide/

Carey, D. (2017). Anchoring sales techniques. Retrieved February 19, 2020 from
   https://smallbusiness.chron.com/anchoring-sales-techniques-21435.html

Carey, T. (2015, August 23). The secret to controlling other people.. Retrieved
   February 8, 2020 from https://www.psychologytoday.com/us/blog/in-
   control/201508/the-secret-controlling-other-people

Carroll, M. (2013). NLP anchoring. Retrieved February 19, 2020 from
   https://www.nlpacademy.co.uk/articles/view/nlp_anchoring/.

Casale, P. (2012). NLP secrets. Retrieved February 14, 2020 from https://www.nlp-
   secrets.com/nlp-secrets-downloads/NLP Secrets.pdf

catherine. (2014, October 9). Introducing frames. *Mind Training Systems*. Retrieved
   February 12, 2020 from
   https://www.mindtrainingsystems.com/content/introducing-frames

Coordinate. (n.d.). In *Lexico*. Retrieved February 18, 2020 from
   https://www.lexico.com/en/definition/coordinate

Ellerton, R. (2008). Meta-model of Milton-model. Retrieved February 16, 2020 from
   http://asbi.weebly.com/uploads/4/4/7/7/4477114/ebook-milton-model-
   summary.pdf.

Ellerton, R. W. (2012). *Win-win influence: How to enhance your personal and business
   relationships*. Renewal Technologies Inc.

Elston, T. (2018). NLP training – The Milton model – Language for change. Retrieved
   February 16, 2020 from https://www.nlpworld.co.uk/nlp-training-the-milton-
   model-language-for-change/

Eng, D. (Ed.). (n.d.). Use NLP to attract a man. Retrieved February 20, 2020 from https://visihow.com/Use_NLP_to_Attract_a_Man

Eye accessing cues. (2019). *NLP World*. Retrieved February 9, 2020 from https://www.nlpworld.co.uk/nlp-glossary/e/eye-accessing-cues/

Firestone, L. (2016). Is your past controlling your life? *Psychology Today*. Retrieved February 8, 2020 from https://www.psychologytoday.com/intl/blog/compassion-matters/201611/is-your-past-controlling-your-life

Frame control: The big secret to starting fun conversations. (n.d.). *Your Charisma Coach*. Retrieved February 14, 2020 from http://www.yourcharismacoach.com/vault/frame-control-the-big-secret-to-starting-fun-conversations/

Frank, M. (2019). 25 secrets of influence and persuasion. *Life Lessons*. Retrieved February 12, 2020 from https://lifelessons.co/personal-development/nlpinfluencepersuasion/

Goldrick, L. (2013). Are covert manipulation techniques ethical? *Common Sense Ethics*. Retrieved February 7, 2020 from https://www.commonsenseethics.com/blog/immorality-of-covert-manipulation-techniques

Golden, B. (2017). Being controlled provokes anger. So does feeling controlled. *Psychology Today*. Retrieved February 8, 2020 from https://www.psychologytoday.com/intl/blog/overcoming-destructive-anger/201706/being-controlled-provokes-anger-so-does-feeling-controlled

Goodman, M. (2018). NLP practitioner notes. Retrieved February 7, 2020 from https://vadea.viaafrika.com/wp-content/uploads/2017/10/NLP-Practitioner-Training-Notes-MD-Goodman.pdf

Grinder, J. & St. Clair, C. B. (n.d.). Is the NLP "Eye Accessing Cues" model really valid? *Bradbury AC*. Retrieved February 9, 2020 from http://www.bradburyac.mistral.co.uk/nlpfax09.htm

Hall, M. (2010). The magic you can perform with reframing. *Neuro-Semantics: International Society of Neuro-Semantics*. Retrieved February 13, 2020 from https://www.neurosemantics.com/the-magic-you-can-perform-with-reframing/

Hartmann, T. (2018). NLP and the power of persuasion - Neuro-linguistic programming [Video file]. *YouTube*. Retrieved February 6, 2020 from https://www.youtube.com/watch?v=sPC2DKswfs0

Henger, K., & Byrne, L. (2019). How to tell if you've offended someone and what you can do to win them over again. *Now to Love*. Retrieved February 10, 2020 from https://www.nowtolove.co.nz/lifestyle/sex-relationships/body-language-how-to-tell-if-youve-offended-someone-win-them-over-again-suzanne-masefield-39815

Home. (n.d.). *Psychoheresy Aware*. Retrieved February 8, 2020 from https://www.psychoheresy-aware.org/nlp-ph.html

How the conscious and subconscious mind work together. (2015). *Mercury*. Retrieved February 14, 2020 from http://www.ilanelanzen.com/mind/how-the-conscious-and-subconscious-mind-work-together/

How you can read people's minds (But not in the way you think). (2017). *Daily NLP*. Retrieved February 9, 2020 from https://dailynlp.com/how-you-can-read-peoples-minds-but-not-in-the-way-you-think/

Hutton, G. (2017). Frame control exercises. *Mind Persuasion*. Retrieved February 13, 2020 from https://mindpersuasion.com/frame-control-exercises/

Hutton, G. (2018, June 6). Milton model. *Mind Persuasion*. Retrieved February 16, 2020 from https://mindpersuasion.com/milton-model/

Iliopoulos, A. (2015). The Russell Brand method - An impressive frame control strategy. *The Quintessential Mind*. Retrieved February 14, 2020 from https://thequintessentialmind.com/the-russel-brand-method/

InspiritiveNLP. (2008). John Grinder discusses what's ethical in NLP [Video file]. Retrieved February 7, 2020 from https://www.youtube.com/watch?v=3pFTMdq0v6Y

Jalili, C. (2019, August 21). How to tell if someone is lying to you, according to experts. *Time*. Retrieved February 11, 2020 from https://time.com/5443204/signs-lying-body-language-experts/

James, G. (2017, May 23). How to instantly reduce stress, according to brain scans. *Inc.*Retrieved February 19, 2020 from https://www.inc.com/geoffrey-james/how-to-instantly-reduce-stress-according-to-science.html

Laborde, G. (2008). Resist hypnosis and hypnotic conversations. *Influence Integrity*. Retrieved February 15, 2020 from https://influence-integrity.blogspot.com/2008/04/resist-hypnosis-and-hypnotic.html

Lawson, C. (2019, January 8). How to seamlessly break down someone's resistance during hypnosis with the non-awareness set. *Hypnosis Training Academy*. Retrieved February 15, 2020 from https://hypnosistrainingacademy.com/break-down-resistance-during-hypnosis/

Ledochowski, I. (2019, October 10). 15 incredibly effective hypnotic power words to ethically influence others - 2nd edition *Hypnosis Training Academy*. Retrieved February 18, 2020 from https://hypnosistrainingacademy.com/3-surefire-power-words-to-gain-power-and-influence-people-fast/

Ledochowski, I. (2019, January 8). 9 essential skills you must master before becoming a seriously skilled conversational hypnotist - 2nd edition. *Hypnosis Training Academy*. Retrieved February 18, 2020 from https://hypnosistrainingacademy.com/becoming-a-great-conversational-hypnotis

Lee, B. (2017, August 15). A weak handshake is worse than no handshake. *Lifehack*. Retrieved February 12, 2020 from https://www.lifehack.org/620939/body-language-deliver-memorable-handshake

Lips body language. (n.d.). *Changing Minds*. Retrieved February 10, 2010 from http://changingminds.org/techniques/body/parts_body_language/lips_body_language.htm

Louv, J. (2017). 10 ways to protect yourself from NLP mind control. *Ultra Culture*. Retrieved February 7, 2020 from https://ultraculture.org/blog/2014/01/16/nlp-10-ways-protect-mind-control

Martin. (2018). Using specifically vague language in your advertising. *Evolution*. Retrieved February 7, 2020 from https://www.evolution-development.com/specifically-vague-language-and-marketing/

Mask, T. (2019). 10 trance signals in covert hypnosis. *Hypnosis Unlocked*. Retrieved February 15, 2020 from https://www.hypnosisunlocked.com/10-trance-signals-in-covert-hypnosis/

Matsumoto, D., & Hwang, H. C. (2018). Microexpressions differentiate truths from liees about future malicious intent. *Frontiers in Psychology*. Retrieved February 12, 2020 from https://www.frontiersin.org/articles/10.3389/fpsyg.2018.02545/full

Mayer, G. (2018). Subconscious mind - How to unlock and use its power. *Thrive Global*. Retrieved February 20, 2020 from https://thriveglobal.com/stories/subconscious-mind-how-to-unlock-and-use-its-power/

Mcleod, A. (2015). Hot words & hot language. *Angus Mcleod*. Retrieved February 18, 2020 from https://angusmcleod.com/hot-words-hot-language

Methods of neuro-linguistic programming. (2019). In *Wikipedia*. Retrieved February 16, 2020 from https://en.wikipedia.org/wiki/Methods_of_neuro-linguistic_programming#Milton_model

Milton Model. (2018). *NLP World*. Retrieved February 15, 2020 from https://www.nlpworld.co.uk/nlp-glossary/m/milton-model/

Mind Tools Co. (2019). NLP eye accessing cues. *Mind Tools*. Retrieved February 9, 2020 from https://www.mindtools.co.th/personal-development/neuro-linguistic-programming/nlp-eye-accessing-cues/

Mind Tools Co. (2019, September 24). NLP anchoring - Feeling good for no reason. *Mind Tools*. Retrieved February 19, 2020 from https://www.mindtools.co.th/personal-development/neuro-linguistic-programming/nlp-anchoring/

MindVale. (2016). NLP hypnosis: how do NLP and hypnosis work together? *Medium*. Retrieved February 14, 2020 from https://medium.com/@mindvale/nlp-hypnosis-how-do-nlp-and-hypnosis-work-together-36e399aa5897

Moghazy, E. (2018). Understanding NLP for healthy relationships. *Marriage.com*. Retrieved February 20, 2020 from https://www.marriage.com/advice/mental-health/understanding-nlp-for-healthy-relationships/

Morris, M. (2017). What is NLP and how do I use it to create success? *Matt Morris*. Retrieved February 6, 2020 from https://www.mattmorris.com/what-is-nlp/

Muoio, D. (n.d.). Body talk: Talk to the hand – The body language of handshakes and hand gestures. *Arch Profile*. Retrieved February 12, 2020 from http://blog.archprofile.com/archinsights/body_language_handshakes_gestures

Newman, S. (2018). Why anyone would want to control you. *Psych Central*. Retrieved February 8, 2020 from https://psychcentral.com/blog/why-anyone-would-want-to-control-you/

NLP Dynamics. (n.d.). Eye accessing cues exercise. *NLP Dynamics*. Retrieved February 9, 2020 from http://www.distancelearning.academy/wp-content/uploads/2015/02/Eye-Accessing-Cues-Exercises.pdf

NLP Milton Model. (2019, May 17). *Excellence Assured*. Retrieved February 16, 2020 from https://excellenceassured.com/nlp-training/nlp-certification/milton-model

NLP skills: Reading eye accessing cues. (2019). *Daily NLP*. Retrieved February 9, 2020 from https://dailynlp.com/eye-accessing-cues/

NLP technique: Framing. (n.d.). *NLP Secrets*. Retrieved February 13, 2020 from https://www.nlp-secrets.com/nlp-technique-framing.php

NLP technique - Positive framing. (n.d.). *NLP Secrets*. Retrieved February 13, 2020 from https://www.nlp-secrets.com/nlp-technique-positive-framing.php

NLP technique: The history of NLP. (n.d.). Retrieved February 9, 2020 from http://www2.vobs.at/ludescher/Grammar/nlp_techniques.htm

NLP today. (n.d.). *NLP School*. Retrieved February 6, 2020 from https://www.nlpschool.com/what-is-nlp/nlp-today/

NLP values, trance words and politics (2015). *The NLP Company*. Retrieved January 7, 2020 from https://www.thenlpcompany.com/mind-control/nlp-values-and-politics/

Non verbal communication. (n.d.). *Maximum Advantage*. Retrieved February 11, 2020 from http://www.maximumadvantage.com/nonverbal-communication/non-verbal-communication-how-to-know-if-someone-is-bored.html

Palokaj, M. (2018). 23 body language tricks that make you instantly likeable. *Lifehack*. Retrieved February 12, 2020 from https://www.lifehack.org/316057/23-body-language-tricks-that-make-you-instantly-likeable

Parvez, H. (2015, May 14). Body language: Positive and negative evaluation gestures. *Psych Mechanics*. Retrieved February 11, 2020 from https://www.psychmechanics.com/positive-and-negative-evaluation/

Quantum-linguistics. (n.d.). *Neurochromatics*. Retrieved February 6, 2020 from https://www.neurochromatics.com/quantum-linguistics/

Radwan, F. (n.d.). Body language: In state of anxiousness. *2 Know Myself*. Retrieved February 11, 2020 from https://www.2knowmyself.com/body_language/body_language_anxious

Radwan, F. (n.d.). Body language: In state of unease, shyness, and defensiveness. *2 Know Myself*. Retrieved February 10, 2020 from https://www.2knowmyself.com/body_language/body_language_defensive_position

Radwan, F. (n.d.). Body language and micro gestures. *2 Know Myself*. Retrieved February 11, 2020 from https://www.2knowmyself.com/Body_language/body_language/micro_gestures

Radwan, F. (n.d.). Body Language & thinking. *2 Know Myself*. Retrieved February 10, 2020 from https://www.2knowmyself.com/body_language/body_language_evaluation

Radwan, F. (n.d.). 5 ways to hypnotize someone during a conversation. *2 Know Myself*. Retrieved February 18, 2020 from https://www.2knowmyself.com/5_ways_to_hypnotize_someone_during_a_conversation

Radwan, F. (n.d.). Reading body language. *2 Know Myself*. Retrieved February 10, 2020 from https://www.2knowmyself.com/body_language/body_language_main

Radwan, F. A. R. O. (n.d.). Using body language to your advantage. *2 Know Myself*. Retrieved February 10, 2020 from https://www.2knowmyself.com/body_language/body_language_reverse

Radwan, M. F. (n.d.). How to convince someone to believe in anything. *2 Know Myself*. Retrieved February 12, 2020 from https://www.2knowmyself.com/Psychology_convincing_someone/Convincing_someone_to_Believe_in_anything

Radwan, F. (n.d.). How to read people's minds (Learn how to read people). *2 Know Myself*. Retrieved February 8, 2020 from https://www.2knowmyself.com/body_language/Mind_Reading/knowing_what_other_people_are_thinking_of

Ready body language. (n.d.). *Changing Minds*. Retrieved February 11, 2020 from http://changingminds.org/techniques/body/ready_body.htm

Self-hypnosis and hypnotherapy. (n.d.). *SkillsYouNeed.com*. **Retrieved February 20, 2020 from https://www.skillsyouneed.com/ps/self-hypnosis.html**

7 most effective mind control techniques tips in NLP. (n.d.). Retrieved February 7, 2020 from https://www.mindorbs.com/article/7-most-effective-mind-control-techniques-tips-nlp

Sewdayal, Y. (2019). Controlling behavior: Signs, causes, and what to do about it. *Supportiv*. Behavior: Signs, Causes, and What To Do About It. Retrieved February 7, 2020 from https://www.supportiv.com/relationships/controlling-behavior-signs-causes-what-to-do

Smith, A. (2018). Introduction to NLP anchoring 8: Chaining anchors. Retrieved February 19, 2020 from https://nlppod.com/nlp-anchoring-chaining-anchors/

Smith, A. (2016). Framing and some commonly used frames in NLP. *Practical NLP Podcast*. Retrieved February 13, 2020 from https://nlppod.com/framing-commonly-used-frames-nlp/

Snyder, D. (2010). Anti-mind control - Building resistance to unethical persuasion and black hypnosis. *NLP Power*. Retrieved February 15, 2020 from https://www.nlppower.com/2010/07/04/anti-mind-control-building-resistance-to-unethical-persuasion-2/

Spector, N. (2018). Smiling can trick your brain into happiness - And boost your health. *NBC News*. Retrieved February 10, 2020 from https://www.nbcnews.com/better/health/smiling-can-trick-your-brain-happiness-boost-your-health-ncna822591

Steber, C. (2017). 11 subtle signs someone may be uncomfortable around you. *Bustle*. Retrieved February 10, 2020 from https://www.bustle.com/p/11-subtle-signs-someone-may-be-uncomfortable-around-you-7662695

Sukhia, R. (2019). Goal setting mindset: The power of autosuggestion and visualization. *Build Business Results*. Retrieved February 20, 2020 from https://buildbusinessresults.com/goal-setting-mindset-the-power-of-autosuggestion-and-visualization/

Sum, Y. (2004). The magic of suggestive language. *Dr. Yvonne Sum*. Retrieved February 15, 2020 from http://www.dryvonnesum.com/pdf/The_Magic_of_Suggestive_Language-NLP.pdf

Sweet, M. (2017). 015 - Learning frames of NLP - And how to apply them. *Mike Sweet*. Retrieved February 13, 2020 from https://www.mikesweet.co.uk/015-learning-frames-nlp/

The body language of confidence. (n.d.). *2 Know Myself*. Retrieved February 12, 2020 from https://www.2knowmyself.com/body_language/body_language_self_confidence

The definitive guide to reading microexpressions (facial expressions). (n.d.). *Science of People*. Retrieved February 12, 2020 from https://www.scienceofpeople.com/microexpressions/

The hypnotic power of words. (2019). *NLP Training Dubai*. Retrieved February 17, 2020 from https://www.nlptrainingdubai.com/the-hypnotic-power-of-words/

The power of NLP. (2018). *Glomacs*. Retrieved February 6, 2020 from https://glomacs.com/articles/the-power-of-nlp

Thomas, A. (2019). NLP in Relationships. *Anil Thomas*. Retrieved February 20, 2020 from https://www.ttgls.in/nlp-relationships/

Tippet, G. (1994). Inside the cults of mind control. *Cult Education*. Retrieved February 7, 2020 from https://culteducation.com/information/8530-inside-the-cults-of-mind-control.html

Tosey, P., & Mathison, J. (1970). NLP and ethics - Outcome, ecology and integrity. *Neuro-Linguistic Programming*, 144-160. https://doi.org/10.1057/9780230248311_12

Tyrrell, I. (2018). The uses and abuses of hypnosis. *Human Givens Institute*. Retrieved February 15, 2020 from https://www.hgi.org.uk/resources/delve-our-extensive-library/ethics/uses-and-abuses-hypnosis

Use autosuggestion techniques to create changes faster. (n.d.). *Wise Goals*. Retrieved February 20, 2020 from https://www.wisegoals.com/autosuggestion-techniques.html

Waude, A. (2016). Emotion and memory: How do your emotions affect your ability to remember information and recall past memories? *Psychologist World*. Retrieved February 19, 2020 from https://www.psychologistworld.com/emotion/emotion-memory-psychology

Westside Toastmasters. (n.d.). The social leverage in active hand gestures. *Westside Toastmasters*. Retrieved February 12, 2020 from https://westsidetoastmasters.com/resources/book_of_body_language/chap2.html

What is covert hypnosis? Discover the 4 stage covert hypnosis formula. (n.d.). *Rebel Magic*. Retrieved February 15, 2020 from https://rebelmagic.com/covert-hypnosis/

Wilcox, D. G. (2011). NLP, mind control, and the arrogance and downfall of power. *Ezine Articles*. Retrieved February 20, 2020 from https://ezinearticles.com/?id=6036132&NLP,-Mind-Control,-and-the-Arrogance-and-Downfall-of-Power=

Woodley, G. (n.d.). Anchoring in sales. *Selling and Persuasion Techniques*. Retrieved February 19, 2020 from https://www.sellingandpersuasiontechniques.com/anchoring-in-sales.html

Wright, S., & Basu, R. (2014). Hypnotic language patterns to bypass resistance. *The NLP Company*. Retrieved February 20, 2020 from https://www.thenlpcompany.com/case-study/hypnotic-language-patterns-to-bypass-resistance/

Your definitive guide to neuro linguistic programming. (2017). *Inner High Living*. Retrieved February 14, 2020 from https://innerhighliving.com/neurolinguistic-programming-guide/

Teaching determiners in articles. (2017, August 11). *Your Dictionary*. Retrieved February 18, 2020 from https://education.yourdictionary.com/for-teachers/teaching-articles-and-determiners.html

Zaharia, C., Reiner, M., & Schütz, P. (2015). Evidence-based neuro linguistic psychotherapy: A meta-analysis. *Psychiatria Danubina, 27*(4), 355-363. https://www.ncbi.nlm.nih.gov/pubmed/26609647

Zhi-peng, R. (2014). Body language in different cultures. *David Publisher*. Retrieved February 10, 2020 from http://www.davidpublisher.com/Public/uploads/Contribute/550928be54286.pdf

EXCLUSIVE GIFT

Hello! Thank you for purchasing this book. Here is your free gift. It's good and it's free!

This mini e-book will answer your questions about this rather controversial skill. It's controversial because it works!

Get ready to learn more about Conversational Hypnosis, simplified for easy and practical use.

Here are just a few of the many benefits of learning Conversational Hypnosis:

- Get your audience to warm up to you and be more open to your message
- Better sales tactics
- Create deeper connections with people
- Create positive change
- And more!

If you want to become a good hypnotic conversationalist, you better start learning the skill today and be a master tomorrow. All you have to do is access the secret download page below.

Open a browser window on your computer or smartphone and enter: <u>bonus.emorygreen.com</u>

You will be automatically directed to the download page.

Remember to influence the world with good intentions.

All the best,
Emory Green

Printed in Great Britain
by Amazon

39998926R00086